A Pocket Guide to

HAWAI'I'S
BOTANICAL
GARDENS

Text by
Kevin Whitton

Photographs by
**Kevin Whitton and
Michelle Whitton**

MUTUAL PUBLISHING

Dedication

This book is dedicated to Solana Lehua Whitton;
may you discover all the beauty life has to offer.

ISBN 10: 1-56647-903-7
ISBN 13: 978-1-56647-903-5

Library of Congress Cataloging-in-Publication Data

Whitton, Kevin J.
  A pocket guide to Hawai'i's botanical gardens / text by Kevin Whitton ; photographs by Kevin
Whitton and Michelle Whitton.
     p. cm.
  ISBN 1-56647-903-7 (softcover : alk. paper)
  1. Botanical gardens--Hawaii--Guidebooks. 2. Hawaii--Guidebooks. I. Whitton, Michelle. II. Title.
III. Title: Hawai'i's botanical gardens.
  QK73.U6W45 2009
  580.7'3969--dc22

                          2009016065

Photos by Kevin Whitton and Michelle Whitton

Design by Kyle Higa

First Printing, July 2009

Mutual Publishing, LLC
1215 Center Street, Suite 210
Honolulu, Hawai'i 96816
Ph: 808-732-1709 / Fax: 808-734-4094
email: info@mutualpublishing.com
www.mutualpublishing.com

Printed in Korea

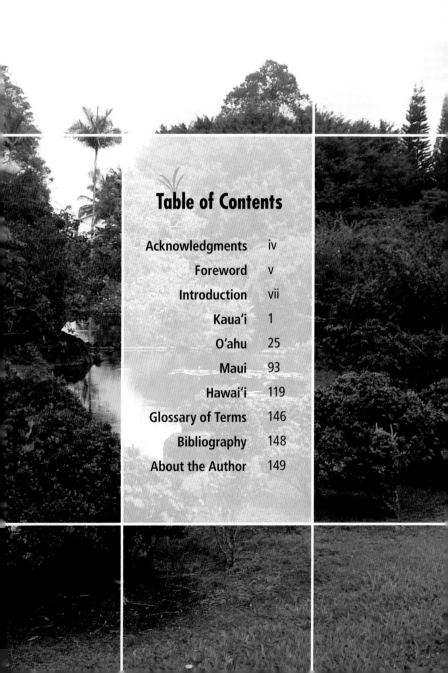

Table of Contents

Acknowledgments

Many thanks go out to the owners, collection managers, directors and organizations that opened up their gardens to me so I could explore, photograph, ponder and in turn, create this guide book. From manini bananas to exotic South American citrus, I was often welcomed with botanical spoils by individuals who were as excited to share their passion for plants and gardens as I was to learn the unique specialties and histories of each garden.

I am also indebted to landscape designer Leland Miyano, who penned the foreword and leads by example with his own amazing, sustainable backyard garden. Leland is a Renaissance man of botany, known for his beautiful botanical installations, his organic and provocative sculptures, his personal research on several native Hawaiian plant species and his knowledge of moving huge boulders with only hand tools. For a gentleman who disdains having to water, his garden is a verdant paradise of native and exotic plants.

And most importantly of all I must thank my wife, Michelle, who continues to give me the love and support to succeed in all my endeavors.

Foreword

Hawai'i is a botanical paradise. Its mild weather and wide range of microclimates is conducive to growing a great multitude of plants. Hawai'i is also a tourist's Mecca; travelers from around the world visit our islands, with many expecting to see a verdant wonderland. In that regard, they will not be disappointed.

When it comes to man, every person on the archipelago now called the Hawaiian Islands (archipelago is a chain of islands) is an immigrant. The original landscape evolved in the absence of man and all the plants were indigenous or endemic. When the Polynesian voyagers came to these islands, the first plant and animal introductions were made. When Westerners re-discovered the islands through the Pacific explorations of Captain Cook, additional introductions were made. Today, plant introductions, whether legal, illegal, intentional or accidental, have increased manyfold. Some of these introductions have become so ubiquitous that they are mistaken for native species. In the lower elevations, it is more likely than not that the plants one sees are not endemic Hawaiian species. People love to grow plants and our residents have surrounded themselves with an amazing selection of species, most of them ornamental and benign exotics. A few of these alien species are classified as invasive species and these are the weedy types that pose the greatest threats to our environment, economy, and society. Hawai'i's original species, the endemics and the indigenous, are under siege by invasive species; this distinction and a sense of bioethics must be learned and embraced.

Hawai'i's botanical gardens are educational places to visit and learn about plants, ecology, landscape design principles, art and a host of other subjects. Botanical gardens can play an important role in conservation and can monitor new imports so invasive species introductions are reduced. It is imperative that non-invasive species have a palatable permitting process so that the illegal importation of plants is not driven further underground. The accredited botanical gardens can play an increased role in this process. Visitors will see a very altered landscape from the original paradise that predated man. These exotic landscapes can be of extraordinary beauty. Looking at those constructed landscapes, we should always remember to be advocates for the preservation and restoration expansion of the remnants of endemic and unique Hawai'i we have remaining. We should not forget that the untouched Hawai'i was truly an Eden without ants, roaches, mosquitoes, termites, rats, snakes, feral goats, or pigs, and the host of species humans associate with vermin. We cannot return to those idyllic times, but moving forward, new species should be introduced with knowledge and responsibility. At this point, it is about finding a new balance in an ever-changing landscape.

All gardens are good starting points for developing a healthy relationship with nature. The resident or visitor will go a long way in their personal growth by seeking out the gardens in this guidebook. Each garden has its own motivation, style, and message, but the love of plants and the celebration of culture are a common thread that weaves them together. The observant and the curious will come away renewed, relaxed, and enlightened by the experiences that each garden uniquely presents. And the deeper and longer one lingers in the exploration, the greater the personal enrichment.

Leland Bryan Miyano

December 3, 2008

Introduction

When I was growing up in Huntington Beach, California, my dad always had some sort of project planned for us on the weekends that entailed being outside in the backyard and working with our hands. We bred rabbits and birds, built terrariums and aviaries, and my favorite, propagated staghorn ferns.

Several ever-expanding clumps of the unique epiphyte adorned the east side of the house. The clumps are actually an assemblage of individual plants growing steadily over one another. When a clump would get too big, reaching its thick and leathery, horned fronds across the narrow pathway toward the house, we would get to work.

My dad would find old pieces of fence post and build small backboards. We would cut up the ferns into individual plants, known as pups, and mount them on a piece of wood with sphagnum moss and green garden tape. Drill a couple holes in the wood and bend up some wire to fashion a hook and violá, a beautifully mounted staghorn fern.

One overgrown fern on the side of the house would yield eight to twelve pups. We'd give them away to friends and neighbors and save a few to spread around our garden. We did this for years and although at the time I was probably anxious to get the work done so I could get a ride to the beach and go surfing, I'm truly thankful for the time I spent with my dad working with those plants in the backyard. It was a precursor to the joy I find getting my hands dirty in the garden.

In college I found myself seeking solace wandering through the prolific nurseries in Santa Barbara, studying the different plants and all too often going home with a few. I began to take notice of landscape architecture and spent a year installing and maintaining koi ponds and water gardens.

My affinity for plants and gardens has grown considerably over the years as I continue to learn about individual plants and the distinct environments and ecosystems in which they thrive. Gardens offer a place of tranquility, clean, oxygen-laden air, and healthy energy, a place to quiet the mind and center the soul. Gardens attract all forms of life and are a reminder that we are but one part of a greater whole, that we share this Earth and these islands with many other creatures that are just as significant as us.

Fortunately, Hawai'i is home to nearly 40 botanical gardens, due in part to our subtropical climate with ample rainfall and steady temperatures. Simply put, most plants grow well in Hawai'i.

The botanical gardens of Hawai'i are as diverse as the plants found growing there; some focus on native Hawaiian plants and Polynesian introductions, some feature fruit trees, some showcase palms and others display colorful tropical foliage and flower displays from around the world. And because of the myriad microclimates found across the islands, dry and arid cactus and succulent gardens are as common as verdant rainforest havens.

So get out there and explore, wander and marvel. Look up at the canopy and look down around your feet. Get up close and personal with delicate, intricate flowers and the varying types of bark on the trunk of a tree, then stand back and take in the whole painting of greens, browns, reds and whites. The rewards are indescribable.

Kaua'i

-  Mosquitoes
- Average Annual Rainfall
- Acres
- Best Known For
- Elevation
- Terrain
- Slippers or Shoes?

Allerton Garden (National Tropical Botanical Garden)

South Shore Visitors Center (Gateway to the Allerton and McBryde Gardens)
4425 Lāwaʻi Road, Kōloa, Hawaiʻi, 96756

Contact: (808) 742-2623 www.ntbg.org/gardens/allerton.php

Directions: From Kaumualiʻi Highway (Hwy 50) turn at the Kōloa/Poʻipū turn-off (Hwy 520). Pass through Kōloa town on Poʻipū Road and turn right from the traffic circle onto Lāwaʻi Road (Spouting Horn turn-off). The entrance is on the right almost two miles ahead, just before the Spouting Horn parking lot.

Hours Daily: Monday – Saturday 9:00 a.m. to 4:30 p.m.

Closed: Sunday

Admission: $40 adult, $20 child (10 to 12 years old), children under 10 not permitted.

Guided Hikes: The two-and-a-half-hour tour includes a 15-minute tram ride and a one-mile walk. Tours commence at 9:00 a.m., 10:00 a.m., 1:00 p.m., and 2:00 p.m. Reservations are required. Call (808) 742-2623 or book online. The Hōʻike Tour is an exclusive three-and-a-half-hour tour of both Allerton and McBryde Gardens. It is offered Tuesday and Wednesday at 8:30 a.m. Adults $85, children (10 to 12 years old) $55, and children under 10 are not permitted. Reservations are required.

Facilities: Restrooms, vending machines, snacks, gift shop.

There is so much interesting history to the Lāwaʻi Valley, both botanical and cultural, that visiting these gardens without a tour guide would be like looking at words on a page of a book and not knowing how to read. That's why Allerton Garden is only accessible via guided tour.

The garden is two miles away from the visitor center, so it's crucial to be on time to meet your tour guide and catch the tram down into the valley. The knowledgeable guides orient you to your surroundings along the tram route, sharing a thorough natural history of the evolution of plants on the Hawaiian Islands and the first peoples to inhabit these fertile islands.

In pre-contact Hawaiʻi, Lāwaʻi Valley was known as the ahupuaʻa (land division) of Lāwaʻi. It was granted to James Young Kanehoa, the son of an advisor to King Kamehameha I, in 1848, who subsequently willed a third of the land to his niece Queen Emma, when he passed away. Kanehoa's widow gave Queen Emma

Most definitely

 ~20 inches

 80 acres

Landscape architecture and secluded beach

Sea level

Level grass and gravel paths

Shoes

Freshwater Lāwaʻi River terminates in verdant Lāwaʻi Bay, where spinner dolphins are known to frequently feed.

the rest of the land in 1885 and Queen Emma took up residence there after her husband and young son passed away. She made plantings of plumeria, bougainvillea, rose apple, mango, pandanus and fern during that time.

During Queen Emma's tenure of the land, she leased the Lāwaʻi Valley to the McBryde family who already owned a great deal of agricultural land in southwest Kauaʻi. The McBryde's eventually bought the valley estate in 1886. At that time the

Pump Six used to deliver water to the upper valley to irrigate thirsty sugarcane fields.

upper valley was planted in sugarcane and the lower valley was planted with taro and rice, farmed by tenant farmers. By 1930, most of the farming in the lower valley had come to a stand still and McBryde sold the lower valley in 1938 to Robert Allerton, an independently wealthy landscape architect from Chicago.

Allerton and his adopted son, John Gregg, also an architect, immediately began expanding the exotic plantings installed by the McBrydes and added themed botanical plantings of their own. Fond of formal gardens, Allerton also incorporated statues, fountains and structures onto his property. During this time Hideo Teshima, who grew up in the valley and was employed in the garden beginning at age 14, worked his way up to become superintendent, a self-taught botanical expert.

In 1964, under petition and urging from Allerton to establish a tropical botanical garden for the United States, the U.S. Congress chartered the Pacific Tropical Botanical Garden. Mr. Allerton made a gift to the virgin institution by purchasing the land farther up the valley, today known as McBryde Garden. Robert Allerton passed away that same year, leaving the property to John Gregg, who lived there till he passed away in 1986. The National Tropical Botanical Gardens Trust took over responsibility of the estate in the early 1990s and Teshima continued to serve as superintendent until he passed in 2001. A palmetum was planted and named in Teshima's honor.

The informative shuttle ride into the valley terminates at Pump Six, the original pump house that delivered water to the sugarcane fields in the upper valley beginning in the early 1900s. The walk on foot begins at the base of a breadfruit tree that stands guard over the quaint house where Teshima grew up. Enter the economic garden filled with ginger, heliconia and calathea. In fact, all subspecies of the banana family are represented here. Spreading monkeypod trees filter the sunlight from above.

From the economic garden, enter Mr. Allerton's Garden of Eden, a work of art that incorporates leaves, flowers, stems and trunks to paint a vision of texture and botanical harmony. Ironically, the fruit tree orchard is first up, but sampling the goods won't have any dire consequences. To the contrary, taste the bittersweet Surinam cherry, the sweet lychee or the bulbous pomelo, just a few of the treats fond in the orchard.

Robert Allerton's spacious "beach cottage."

The tour continues under tall and lanky African tulip trees and up onto a site with an Italian logia and Romanesque female statue on a stone pedestal separated by a reflection pool. Robert Allerton originally requested that Diana on the Hunt stand guard over the reflective pool, but on her overseas arrival, it was clear that the statue was not Diana, but an even more fitting accompaniment to the surrounding foliage.

Twisting, warping limbs from an old kiawe tree loom overhead as you head to the next section in the garden, once again graced with water. A long, three-tiered reflection pool dissects the planting of Macarthur palms and bird's nest anthurium, the largest of all anthuriums. Tucked away in between the delicate green foliage is Robert Falls, a seemingly natural tumbling waterfall that John Gregg design and installed for Robert in just under a week while he was away.

A corridor of red torch ginger and other heliconia lead to the snaking, buttressed trunks of three Morerton Bay fig trees, the same featured in the Hollywood film Jurassic Park. The giant canopy trees were collected as saplings in Australia by Allerton and sent back to Hawai'i in empty beer cans. Planted in 1952, they now dominate the bank of the Lāwa'i Stream that meanders through the garden to Lāwa'i Bay.

above: There are many interesting fountains throughout Allerton Garden. This curious design causes the water to pulse at 60 beats per minute as it empties into its receiving vesicle. below: Bamboo can grow up to 12 inches a day.

On the left, past the fig trees, is another European installation, a long, narrow cement culvert fountain with a figurine statue at each end. The fountain is one long, continuous wavelength with mahogany blocks placed at the troughs of each wave. The blocks cause the single stream to pulsate as it falls into a shallow bowl at 60 beats per minute. The auditory effect subconsciously slows the heartbeat to relax the mind to even further enjoy the garden.

The tour continues along the riverbank, past a vast stand of yellow and green striped bamboo and the Allerton guesthouse, which is now used to accommodate researchers at the garden, and on to a grassy lawn with fine, white sand just 50 feet away. There is no better place to wake up every morning, so it's no surprise to find Allerton's "beach cottage" and Queen Emma's cottage overlooking the tranquil and secluded Lāwaʻi Bay. Keep your eyes peeled for spinner dolphins that frequent the well-stocked shallows.

A bridge crosses the river, past a natural circular volcanic mound used in day's past to spot schools of fish in the bay, and violá, another shuttle awaits to gingerly assist you back to the visitor center. The return trip cuts through the riparian, an outdoor classroom of plants designed for study planted along the riverbank, an ethnobotanical bastion of research and learning. It also dissects the palmetum, a collection of over 200 feather and fan palms including native loulu palms, cycads and Hideo's hybrid hibiscus collection.

The tour of the Allerton Garden is an all encompassing, tangible experience that titillates the mind and calms the soul. But this is not the only tour available. There is also a sunset tour that incorporates a catered meal at sunset on the lawn in front of the beach house and the all inclusive, two-garden Hōʻike Tour. This behind-the-scenes tour visits Allerton and McBryde gardens, starting with the exploration of a secluded waterfall trail, a private excursion of the Conservation and Horticulture Center as well as the micropropagation lab and an in depth look at Allerton's palmetum and riparian. The three-and-a-half hour tour includes water, juice and snacks.

Traditionally, fishermen used the mount on the other side of Lāwaʻi River as a vantage point to spot schools of fish in the bay.

Limahuli Garden and Preserve
(National Tropical Botanical Garden)

Hā'ena, Hawai'i 96714

Contact: (808) 826-1053 garden, (808) 332-7324 administration
www.ntbg.org/gardens/limahuli.php

Directions: Take the Kuhio Highway (Hwy 560) north. Pass through Hanalei. Limahuli Garden is located in Hā'ena, one-half mile past mile marker 9.

Hours Daily: Tuesday – Saturday 9:30 a.m. to 4:00 p.m.

Closed: Sunday and Monday

Admission: Self-guided tours: $15 adults, children 12 and under are free. Guided tours: $25 adults, $15 10–18 years old, children under 10 not allowed.

Guided Hikes: One-and-a-half-hour self-guided tours begin at 9:30 a.m. and two-and-a-half-hour guided tours begin at 10:00 a.m. Reservations are required for guided tours. Call (808) 826-1053 or make reservations online.

Facilities: Restrooms, water fountains, snacks, complimentary walking sticks, mosquito repellent, umbrellas and ponchos. No picnicking and no smoking.

Chartered with similar mission and purpose of Kahanu Garden on Maui, this National Tropical Botanical Garden strives to preserve and perpetuate the knowledge of native plants as well as native Hawaiian culture. Limahuli Garden and Preserve is not only a botanical garden set inside the dramatic Limahuli Valley, but also natural preserve with ongoing native forest restoration, riparian (stream bank) restoration throughout the valley and lo'i restoration at the coast.

Limahuli Valley was originally part of the ahupua'a of Hā'ena in ancient Hawai'i. A thriving ancient living site due to the abundance of fresh water, the surrounding forests remained in pristine conditions until the early 1900s, when cattle grazing denuded parts of the valley and invasive plant species took hold. In a recent turn of events, the forest has become choked with schefflera, the octopus tree, which appeared in the valley as a result of Hurricane Iniki in 1992.

With the mountain peaks of Pōhaku-o-Kāne, Makana and its neighboring needles Mauna Hou and Mauna Puluo keeping watch over the valley, the valley

Terraced loʻi kalo at the mouth of Limahuli Valley.

left: Kalo was a staple food source for ancient Hawaiians living in the Hāʻena ahupuaʻa.
right: A stop to relax under a kukui tree.

has retained much of its cultural history and essence, due in part because the valley was never used for large-scale sugarcane production despite its abundance of fresh water.

And fresh water is one of the major themes that permeates the garden, apparent right away in the Canoe Garden, the first plantings you'll come upon at Limahuli. Functioning stone terraced loʻi kalo, carbon-dated at 700 years old, hold taro, the ancient Hawaiians most important crop. The agriculture system works today as it did hundreds of years ago, naturally fed by Limahuli Stream and flowing by gravity down the terraces, then back to the main stream channel.

Cliffs rise sharply on both sides of the valley as you wind your way up the terraces and through the Canoe Garden, with sweet potato, 'awa, ti, banana, noni, 'awapuhi (shampoo ginger) and other canoe plants beset by native ferns and shaded by kukui trees. The fragrant scent of tiare, Polynesian gardenia wafts by on the breeze.

Hibiscus, croton and other tropical flowering ornamentals mark the Plantation Garden of exotic tropical plants. The sound of rushing water wonderfully overwhelms the verdant setting as smaller streams crisscross the main trail and the main channel rushes past smooth boulders. Kukui trees and hala line the stream banks, the long tough leaves of the pandanus hang and flitter over the cool moving water. The serenity is intoxicating and the garden exudes calming vibrations.

Where the main road crosses the stream, stay to the left and climb the stairs to quickly gain elevation. Walk through the stone remains of an ancient living site and continue on to the Native Forest Walk. In this section of the garden, the invasive species that once dominated this swath of forest have been removed and only native Hawaiian species were replanted. This reforestation demonstrates what a healthy native forest should look like, with ground covers, ferns and shrubs, small trees comprising an understory and larger canopy trees over top, complete with epiphytes and vines throughout. Many of the plants along the walk are endangered species and very rare in the wild. Native northwest Kaua'i plants are also accounted for here. Mamaki shrubs are naturalizing in the forest, meaning they

left: Makana towers above Limahuli Valley. right: Limahuli Stream brings water from high in the mountains to the lo'i kalo below.

left: Kukui trees and hala fringe Limahuli Stream. right: Stone remnants of the ancient living site.

are sprouting naturally from seed and palapali'i grass is abundant. Loulu palms, koa trees, and sitting benches line the dirt path.

Up next is the Invasive Forest Walk, a stark reminder of what happens when aggressive invasive species out compete sensitive natives and take over the forest. Notice that the diversity is nearly gone from this forest. Only five species of trees exist here: the autograph tree, schefflera (octopus or umbrella tree), strawberry guava and java plum have blocked nearly all the sunlight from reaching the barren forest floor and the forest is choked with thin, narrowly spaced tree trunks. Unfortunately, this is the state of much of Hawai'i's forests. The difference is so striking when they are situated side by side as in this garden.

Emerge from under the canopy of invasives and marvel at the view of the Pacific Ocean from your elevated vantage point with beautiful koa trees in the foreground. A maintenance road curves downhill to the left, but stay on the path to the right and skirt along the mountainside, through the many native plantings that thrive on the grassy slope. One success story found throughout this area is the ālula, an unusual squatty Kaua'i and Ni'ihau native with lobey leaves and small flowers protruding from the top of bulbous, thick and fleshy trunks. Some say it looks like cabbage growing out of the top of a baseball bat. Thought to be extinct in the wild due to the loss of its native pollinator, a night moth, endangered ālula has made such a comeback in cultivation it can be found in nurseries. The plant has been actively propagated and outplanted and thanks to a new pollinator (ants), the ālula is close to coming off the endangered species list.

The white hibiscus, koki'o ke'oke'o, endemic to northwest Kaua'i is planted across this mountain meadow as well. Another plant thought to be extinct, Limahuli Preserve staff discovered 30-foot tall trees of the dainty, white-flowered hibiscus, growing at the very back of the valley.

A lone pandanus, or hala as its known in Hawaiian, marks the high point of the walk. Mature 'ōhi'a lehua trees mark your descent down easily navigated switchbacks to the lo'i terraces below.

left: The Native Forest Walk passes by thriving native ferns. right: A spectacular view of the Pacific Ocean from the highpoint of the garden.

McBryde Garden (National Tropical Botanical Garden)

South Shore Visitors Center (Gateway to the Allerton and McBryde Gardens)
4425 Lāwaʻi Road, Kōloa, Hawaiʻi, 96756

Contact: (808) 742-2623 www.ntbg.org/gardens/allerton.php

Directions: From Kaumualiʻi Highway (Hwy 50) turn at the Kōloa/Poʻipū turn-off (Hwy 520). Pass through Kōloa town on Poʻipū Road and turn right from the traffic circle onto Lāwaʻi Road (Spouting Horn turn-off). The entrance is on the right almost two miles ahead, just before the Spouting Horn parking lot.

Hours Daily: 9:00 a.m. to 4:00 p.m.

Admission: Self-guided tours: $20 adult, $10 child (6 to 12 years old), children 5 years and under are free. Guided Tour: $40 adult, $20 child (10 to 12 years old), children under 10 not permitted.

Guided Hikes: All tours require a round-trip, 15-minute tram ride. One-and-a-half-hour self-guided tours commence hourly Monday through Saturday, beginning at 9:30 a.m. and the last tour leaving at 2:30 p.m. On Sunday, self-guided tours are available at 11:30 a.m., 12:30 p.m., 1:30 p.m. and 2:30 p.m. and a guided tour is offered at 9:00 a.m. Self-guided tours are on a first come, first served basis, no reservations are accepted. Reservations are required for the guided Sunday morning tour. Call (808) 742-2623 or book online. The Hōʻike Tour is an exclusive three-and-a-half-hour tour of both McBryde and Allerton Gardens. It is offered Tuesday and Wednesday at 8:30 a.m. Adults $85, children (10 to 12 years old) $55, and children under 10 are not permitted. Reservations are required.

Facilities: Restrooms, vending machines, snacks, gift shop.

McBryde Garden is situated in the upper Lāwaʻi Valley and is the first of the National Tropical Botanical Gardens, established in 1970. Part of the original ahupuaʻa of Lāwaʻi, the land came down through several hands before Duncan McBryde purchased the property that he had been leasing from Queen Emma in 1886. The upper valley was home to a large-scale sugar operation, the McBryde Sugar Company.

The plantation is long gone, along with the thirsty sugarcane, and in its place is an amazingly diverse collection of exotic and native plants. Originally named the Lāwaʻi Garden, the Lāwaʻi Stream meanders the length of the garden and con-

Oh yeah

~20 inches

252 acre garden, tour encompasses 24 acres

Native palm collection

20 to 50 feet

Level gravel and dirt paths with inclines, stairs and a grassy meadow

Shoes

tinues through Allerton Garden and out into Lāwaʻi Bay. This perennial flow and the deep and wide valley create a wealth of microclimates, from meadow to cliff and cool stream bank to hot and dry plateau. The verdant spectacle is breathtaking and the right combination for a wealth of different plants.

A tram ride is required to access the garden and the driver or your tour guide will get you up to speed on the natural and cultural history of the area. Don't miss the medicinal plants section, which is used for research purposes. It's not open to the public because of the toxicity of many of the plants and trees, so this is your only glimpse at them. The tram deposits you at the rear of the valley near the Canoe Garden and a newly constructed restroom with drinking fountains.

left: A gazebo offers shade and a view of a small pond after walking through the Canoe Garden. right: The hanging fruit of the endangered Munroidendron racemosum.

The Canoe Garden showcases plants of ancient Polynesia, the useful plants that the first Polynesian settlers brought to Hawaiʻi in their canoes. Past the gazebo in the garden is a small pond under the partial canopy of a monkeypod tree. There is an ʻalae ʻula, native Hawaiian moorhen, that frequents the lily pond.

Cross the stream and find yourself at the head of the valley, tall and mature exotic trees all around. The Lāwaʻi Stream flows down one side of the meadow and along its banks is the majority of the canopy. Several different types of loulu palm line the other side of the meadow, below the road, planted amongst other Kauaʻi natives like the white hibiscus and the curious *Munroidendron racemosum*, endemic to Kaua'i and very rare in the wild, so rare, that its Hawaiian name has been lost over time.

In fact, McBryde Garden has the largest assemblage of native Hawaiian plants of all the National Tropical Botanical Gardens. This is not by accident: the garden also doubles as a research and education facility with micropropagation lab and

top: A path through the Reading Palms. left: The bamboo bridge will add a spring to your step. right: The cool, shaded banks of upper Lāwa'i Stream.

the Conservation and Horticulture Center. Scientists from all over the world come to study at the gardens and local botanists continue to bolster populations of native species for restoration work.

To educate the public, McBryde Garden offers A Walk Among the Natives section on a drier plateau across from the meadow. This planting is a cross section of important native species, from ground covers to trees. Follow the loop trail and keep your eyes peeled for the threatened wiliwili, or coral tree.

Back down in the meadow, following the stream and tall trees, the valley bottlenecks and the climate immediately cools as the valley becomes narrow and deep around the streambed. The canopy conceals much of the sunlight and the plants reflect that environmental change. Here you'll find the Reading Palms, a palmetum, or collection of palms, used for conservation, research and education. Of the original 23 native loulu palm species across the Hawaiian Islands, only 15 remain and all can be found at this garden.

Make your way down stream, past heliconia, ginger, calathea and ferns to the bamboo bridge. On the other side of the bridge is a loop trail that ascends through the Spice of Life planting, introduced economic plants, and takes a stop at the eloquent Maidenhair Falls, also known as Waihulili Falls.

Back on the main trail that parallels the stream, continue downstream under the shade of canopy trees filled with epiphytes like staghorn ferns, orchids and bromeliads, until you come to the tram road and pickup locale.

left: Spacious upper Lāwaʻi Valley was once planted in sugarcane. Now it's a vast meadow. right: Up the stone steps and through the Spice of Life planting to Waihulili Falls.

Moir Garden

2253 Po'ipū Road, Po'ipū, Hawai'i 96756

Contact: (808) 742-6411

Directions: From Kaumauali'i Highway (Hwy 50) turn at the Kōloa/Po'ipū turn-off (Hwy 520). Pass through Kōloa town on Po'ipū Road and follow the sign at the traffic circle to Po'ipū. The Outrigger Kiahuna Plantation is on the right directly across from the Po'ipū Shopping Village. Moir Garden is located on the grounds of the Outrigger Kiahuna Plantation.

Hours Daily: Everyday during daylight hours.

Closed: After dusk

Admission: Free

Guided Hikes: Only self-guided walks at this garden.

Facilities: Restrooms located inside the Plantation Gardens restaurant.

Yup, repellent is neccessary

~20 inches

1.5 acres

Succulents

Sea level

Level, but narrow gravel paths

Slippers

Moir Garden is a labor of love, and a thorny one at that. This landscaping of succulents, cactus, bromeliads, orchids and drought tolerant trees was the creation of Alexandra "Sandie" Moir and designed back in the 1930s. Her husband, Hector Moir, was the plantation manager of the nearby Kōloa Plantation, Hawai'i's first sugar plantation. The garden is just footsteps away from the Moirs' single story plantation home, now known as the Plantation Gardens Restaurant, which was a wedding gift to the couple from Sandie's father.

Some stories say that Sandie brought many of the succulents and cacti from their previous home in Arizona, while others rumor that most of the plants were obtained through early mail order. Either way, some the drought tolerant plants in this

top left: Moir Garden is a sea of succulents. top right: There is a lovely orchid garden on the side of the Plantation Garden restaurant, part of the Moir's original plantation home. bottom left: Standing water is not the first thing you think of in a cactus garden, but the lily pond offers colorful blooms among thorny limbs. bottom right: A sprinkle of color.

garden are nearly 100 years old. Mrs. Moir's hobby quickly turned into a rich botanical undertaking as she continued to add plants over the years.

When you turn into the resort parking lot, immediately look for a place to park and walk to the Plantation Garden Restaurant, which is just the behind the guest registration. Both are located in the Moir's plantation home. A bright and airy orchid garden accentuates the path around the house. Cross the grass in front of the home's spacious lanai and you'll see the sign for Moir garden up ahead, between two wiliwili trees.

The garden has multiple trails that crisscross and loop through the plantings of succulents. Half the fun is finding what's in bloom during your walk. There are only a couple signs, so relax and admire the beauty of the mature garden.

Dominated by agave and aloe, it goes without saying that the garden has a desert feel, especially with Po'ipū's dry and sunny climate. African tulip trees

top: Sometimes you have to get up close to find the hidden treasure. bottom left: Several condominiums border the garden. bottom right: Succulents thrive in Po'ipū's dry coastal climate.

hem in the far end of the garden, planted by two condominiums on the other side of the spiky and fleshy landscape.

There are several flowering trees in the garden, but there is little shade. Oddly enough, there is a lily pond in the center of the garden, a sort of mirage in the desert, and brightly colored flowers pop open above green floating platforms.

Some of the pathways, especially toward the back of the garden, get thick between the plants, with different cactus popping up all around. While you're there, make sure you check out *Euphorbia neglecta*, a mass of limbs tumbling over each other like spaghetti, twisting and bulging, motley appendages hanging from several elusive trunks.

In Poʻipū's dry climate, this unique garden seems very much at home. The lichen covered lava rocks add a great contrast to the sea of pointy green, serrated leaves and spiny arrangement on fleshy columnar stocks. The Moir's named their home and garden "Paʻu a Laka," or skirt of Laka, after the Hawaiian goddess of Hula and the Hawaiian name for the area.

left: Euphorbia neglecta *in the background definitely looks like it's mangled and neglected. right: With thorns around every corner, watch your step and move slowly through Moir Garden.*

Na 'Āina Kai Botanical Garden

P.O. Box 1134, 4101 Wailapa Road, Kīlauea, Hawai'i 96754

Contact: (808) 828-0525 www.naainakai.org info@naainakai.org

Directions: From the Kuhio Highway (Hwy 560) turn onto Wailapa Road, which is in between mile markers 21 and 22. Look for the iron gate at the end of the half-mile road.

Hours Daily: Monday (Orchid House Visitor Center and Gift Shop only) 8:00 a.m. to 2:00 p.m., Tuesday – Thursday 8:00 a.m. to 5:00 p.m., Friday 8:00 a.m. to 1:00 p.m.

Closed: Weekends and holidays

Admission: $30 to $75 based on length of guided tour, discounted rates for Hawai'i residents.

Guided Hikes: All tours are guided and offered Tuesday through Friday for children 13 years of age or older. The five different tours range in length from one-and-a-half to five hours. Reservations are recommended, but they do accept walk-in guests on a space-available basis. Special family tours are offered for children younger than 13 and reservations are required. Call (808) 828-0525 or email reservations@ naainakai.org.

Facilities: Clean restrooms, visitor center, Orchid House Gift Shop, Bamboo Gallery, water fountains, beverages for sale, and complimentary tea and coffee.

Weddings: Contact events@naainakai.org for information about planning weddings and other functions.

What started out as a backyard garden for Joyce and Ed Doty in 1982 has blossomed into a landscaped botanical creation with several themed gardens surrounding a man-made lagoon, one of the largest bronze sculpture collections in the U.S., a secluded beach, and a hardwood plantation of 60,000-plus trees. Whether you choose to tour the garden on foot, by motorized carriage, or both, the garden offers unique and visually pleasing landscaping around every bend.

Na 'Āina Kai's Primary Garden is a flowing distribution of at least six other smaller themed gardens, blended by foliage and flower. Exotic plants and Polynesian introductions line a streambed that meanders across the 240-acre property and is referred to as the Wild Garden. The majority of the land is methodically planted in rows of exotic hardwoods and is known as the Kilohana Hardwood Plantation.

Not too bad

 ~84 inches

 240 acres

Bronze sculptures and hardwood groves

Sea level to 220 feet

Level grass, gravel and cement paths on mid-length tours. Inclined dirt trails on 5-hour tour

Slippers for the covered motorized carriage tours and short walks, and shoes for the long hikes.

Rows upon rows of teak, Tectona grandis, *a sought after hardwood.*

Bronze sculptures have been strategically placed throughout the Primary Garden and Wild Garden. A Horticulture Amusement Garden is in the works, planted with edible fruits for tasting and unusual ornamentals.

In the Primary Garden, you might think the International Desert Garden is somewhat out of place on Kaua'i's wet and rainy north shore. But the Dotys have overcome the excess moisture with extremely well draining soil. Cacti and suc-

left: "Valentine" by George Lundeen. right: "The Big Fish Story" by Paul Baliker.

The International Desert Garden is a desert oasis in the middle of a tropical paradise. With special mounds of well-draining soil, many different species of cacti and succulents can thrive in the moist environment.

culents are planted across hills of soil, with drought tolerant trees, like the squatty tamarind, creating a low umbrella over the hilltop. Bromeliads and aloe are also found in abundance in this area.

The cactus garden pushes up against the palm garden, with palms and cycads from around the world. The palm garden leads to a vine-covered residence, the Dotys' original house, which is now used mainly for weddings and private parties.

The Islands of Flavor is an edible spice garden next to the cliffside abode. Cardamom, cinnamon, basil, oregano, rosemary, sweet tapioca and allspice mingle on the breeze for olfactory bliss. A row of plumeria trees across from the spice garden leads to the Poinciana Maze, aptly named because of the spreading, thick canopy of a royal Poinciana tree and a statue of a young lady relaxing on a swing in the shade beneath the foliage. The maze is not a puzzle, but two mirror-image halves. Statues are the draw here. There are 15 throughout the maze and a few topiaries to match. Interestingly, 2,400 mock orange plants make up the rectangular hedge.

Across from the maze is Ka'ula Lagoon. Once again, statuary dominates the landscaping around the lagoon, but is incorporated into the botanical landscape as accents to a particular setting, not the main focus. Paths encircle the garden and stairs lead up to a Japanese teahouse and waterfall setting. Behind the teahouse is Shower Tree Park, where staghorn ferns, orchids and bromeliads accent the thick limbs of shower trees and several statues dot the lawn.

How much of the entire garden you see depends solely on which of the five tours you choose to take. The Primary Garden is included in every tour, but you'll have to venture out to see the Wild Garden, the hardwood plantation, or Kuliha'ili Canyon that leads down to Kaluakai Beach at the Makai Meadow and Marsh. The tours also offer different options of walking and riding the motorized carriage.

Na 'Āina Kai also has a garden for the kids, the "Under The Rainbow" Children's Garden. Complete with a 16-foot Jack and the Beanstalk sculpture and fountain, kids can get wet, cool off, run around and check out the tropical jungle with bridges, tunnels and slides among other activities.

left: Cardamom flower. right: Plants and sculpture interact throughout the garden; "Lively Encounter" by Kay Worden with a bed of zinnias.

O'ahu

- Mosquitoes
- Average Annual Rainfall
- Acres
- Best Known For
- Elevation
- Terrain
- Slippers or Shoes?

The Contemporary Museum Gardens

2411 Makiki Heights Drive, Honolulu, Hawai'i 96822

Contact: toll free (866) 991-2835, (808) 526-1322, www.tcmhi.org

Directions: Drive mauka (toward the mountains) on Punahou Street, turn left on Nehoa Street, turn right on Makiki Street, at the first small intersection turn left onto Makiki Heights Drive. Go about a mile up the hill and the museum entrance is on the right.

Hours Daily: Tuesday – Saturday: 10:00 a.m. to 4:00 p.m. Sunday: noon to 4:00 p.m.

Closed: Mondays, New Year's Day, Easter Day, Fourth of July, Thanksgiving and Christmas.

Admission: Adults $8, seniors and students with valid ID $6, members and children under 12 are free, retired, active, reserve military and their families are free with military IDs, free to the public on the third Thursday of each month, free admission to The Contemporary Museum Café and The Museum Shop.

Guided Hikes: Guided garden tours by request, call the education department at (808) 237-5230.

Facilities: Restrooms, drinking fountains, museum, The Contemporary Museum Café and The Museum Shop.

The farther down the valley, their numbers increase exponentially

~50 inches

3.5 acres

Terraced Japanese stroll garden

375 to 405 feet

Compact dirt and gravel trails with stone steps

Shoes

Even without knowing the remarkable history of this garden, at first glance it's obvious that a lot of love, contemplation, consideration and hard work went into the planning and landscaping of this expertly arranged botanical wonder. The garden, known as Nu'umealani or heavenly terrace, fills a long-since barren ravine with over 80 species of flowering plants, tree, palms and tropical botanicals. Strategically arranged rocks and paths with handmade stone steps guide visitors on a botanical adventure, where the garden unfolds harmoniously around each bend.

Originally landscaped between 1928 and 1941 by Reverend K.H. Inagaki, he designed the garden incorporating the Japanese doctrine of shizen, or nature, by utilizing rocks in every aspect, from func-

left: The Contemporary Museum Garden incorporates ground covers, shrubs and flowering plants under a well-established canopy. right: The smooth, mottled bark of the lemon-scented gum.

tion to aesthetics, creating a garden with natural qualities and geological subtleties. Inagaki selected each and every rock and carefully arranged and placed them throughout the garden. Even more amazing is that he did this all from his wheelchair after a serious auto accident.

Inagaki created the terraced garden to compliment the residence, built by Anna Rice Cooke, widow of Charles Montague Cooke, which housed and displayed her collection of Asian and European art. Her daughter, Alice Spalding, and her husband, Philip, inherited the property and continued the tradition of supporting the arts. Mrs. Spalding donated the Cooke-Spalding residence after she died to the Honolulu Academy of Arts. In 1979 it was bought by a private developer and sold to a company owned by another artistically-minded individual, Thurston Twigg-Smith, who then generously gave the property to the community for the benefit of local contemporary artists. In 1988, The Contemporary Museum opened to the public and the gardens have since been available for public viewing, with updated plantings focusing on native Hawaiian botanicals.

Much care was taken in designing the paths, which control the direction and progress through the garden, introducing new botanical delights around every turn. The top of the ravine is shaded by a canopy of kukui trees, monkeypod, white monkeypod with its ashen mottled trunk, eucalyptus, mock orange and

left: The Contemporary Museum is visible through the foliage in the upper portion of the garden. right: A stone bench offers a place to sit and relax.

The lower portion of the garden is heavily shaded and features interesting rock formations.

O'ahu

macadamia nut. Only part of the ravine unfolds below until you start down one of the several winding paths.

Bromeliads, ferns, calathea and many other flowering groundcovers leave no inch of soil in the quiet valley bare. While walking down, the left side is cloaked in heliconia, ginger, bamboo and a planting of Chinese fan palms. Heavily shaded, the mosquitoes seem to congregate in this area. The opposite side of the verdant valley is thickly covered in monstera with splaying, spade-shaped green foliage. The main trail on the right side of the ravine terminates with beautiful views of Honolulu and the Pacific Ocean under the thick lobe leaves of an autograph tree.

At the bottom of the ravine, ficus trees spread their canopy wide and block the piercing overhead sun. Their advantageous roots cover much of the ground and snake down moist rock walls. Curiously-shaped moss-covered rocks adorn the swirling end of the path. Standing alone and positioned to evoke geological formations, the rocks lead you back into a cave-like area, a natural shelter, calm and peaceful. At every turn, the garden has the ability to transport the wanderer to a botanical world of harmony and delight.

left: Heliconia pendula *inflorescence. right: Stone stairs lead to the bottom of the sun-dappled ravine.*

East-West Center Japanese Garden and Friendship Circle and Garden

1601 East-West Road, Honolulu, Hawai'i, 96848

Contact: (808) 944-7204 www.eastwestcenter.org

Directions: From the H-1 East exit University Avenue, turn right onto University Avenue, turn right on Dole Street, turn left onto East-West Road. Visitor parking is located behind Kennedy Theater off East-West Road or in the parking structure on Dole Street.

Hours Daily: 24 hours a day

Admission: Free

Guided Hikes: Not available

Facilities: Not available

Just a few in the Japanese Garden

40 inches

Less than 3 acres combined

Japanese Garden

~108 feet

Gravel pathways, flagstone stairs and level grass

Take your pick

The East-West Center, adjacent to the University of Hawai'i at Mānoa campus in lower Mānoa Valley, hosts two gardens, both unique in their own right. The Friendship Circle and Garden is a quiet and calm place to sit and relax or stroll along the snaking path. It is located between Hale Mānoa and John A. Burns Hall, on the east side of East-West Road. Designed by Umemoto Cassandro Design Corporation and local landscape designer Leland Miyano, the two-acre garden was completed in 2003.

The simple garden offers a quiet respite from the bustle of campus and a shady spot to sit and relax. Two mature ficus trees flank the Friendship Circle and their intermingling canopies shade the native basalt stone circular courtyard. On each side of the circle, waist-high rock walls create an outline of the circle and conceal basalt stone benches. A grassy lawn fades back toward Hale Halawai and is bordered with native white hibiscus. Mature plumeria and young kukui trees offer shade on the manicured lawn.

top: Mature ficus trees provide ample shade. left: Native white hibiscus borders the garden. right: Stone benches are seamlessly incorporated into the stone borders.

Fern and mondo grass soften the landscape around the buttressed trunks of the ficus trees and native and Polynesian plants line a walking path and a meandering trail that winds away from the Friendship Circle.

The center's other botanical wonder is the Japanese Garden, complete with teahouse, waterfalls and schools of large koi fish. Located behind the Hawaiʻi Imin

left: Path to the Jakuan Teahouse. right: The Jakuan Teahouse was presented to the University of Hawai'i by the 15th generation grand tea master of Urasenke Konnichian, Mr. Soshitsu Sen.

International Conference Center, the Japanese Garden was created in 1963, shortly after the U.S. Congress established the East-West Center in 1960. The garden was a gift from a group of Japanese business officials in 1963 and a collaboration of specialists from Asia, the Pacific and the United States.

From the teahouse at the top of a hill, the garden falls away quickly down a steep slope and a trail of stone steps leads garden enthusiasts around the botanical collection. Tall and mature strawberry guava trees with smooth, hard trunks surround the teahouse and provide a good amount of shade. The trail snakes around the short manicured umbrella of Japanese tobira trees and the under the canopy of a pink shower tree (coral tree), which was planted by then Prince Akihito and Princess Michiko of Japan on May 16, 1964. Princess Michiko also blessed the garden when the koi were introduced into the stream.

A stream dissects the garden. Beginning near the teahouse, a waterfall showers koi in a pond up stream. The water flows naturally down rocks and rivets, separating and merging at the bottom of the hill into the s-curved stream that continues the length of the garden. The stream is said to represent a river flowing from the mountains to the city to the sea, and is fashioned after the Japanese Kanji character for "heart." A majority of the colorful koi idly pace the lower and deeper region of the stream.

The stream is beset by a large monkeypod, shadowing a red bottlebrush or weeping callistemon, planted by the Prime Minister of Japan Zenko Suzuki on June 16, 1982. The scene is completed with a stone pagoda perched on a stone overlooking the riverbank. Expanses of grass line both sides of the stream.

left: From the teahouse to the stream below, there are several small waterfalls with koi fish in each pond. right: Stone steps lead from the teahouse to the meandering stream and lawn area below.

The garden is exceptionally well maintained and manicured. In the foreground is Pittosporum tobira, *behind it the stream snakes away.*

Foster Botanical Garden (Honolulu Botanical Gardens)

50 N. Vineyard Blvd., Honolulu, Hawai'i 96817

Contact: (808) 522-7066, www.co.honolulu.hi.us/parks/hbg/fbg.htm

Directions: On the mauka side (mountain side) of Vineyard in between Nu'uanu Avenue and A'ala Street.

Hours Daily: 9:00 a.m. to 4:00 p.m.

Closed: Christmas Day and New Year's Day

Admission: Adults $5 (13 and older), kama'āina $3, children $1 (6-12 years old), free for children 5 and under, $25 for an annual family pass.

Guided Hikes: Free. Monday through Saturday at 1 p.m. Other tours can be arranged upon request.

Facilities: Bookstore, gift shop, art gallery, restrooms.

Weddings: Permit required

Not a problem	
30 to 40 inches	
13.5 acres	
Exceptional trees	
12 to 43 feet	
Level grass, dirt, gravel and cement	
Slippers	

Foster Botanical Garden is a verdant expanse of flora nestled inbetween Chinatown and the bustling H1 interstate freeway. Chances are you've driven past it without even knowing it's there. For nature lovers, that might not sound too appealing, but once you pass through the dense vegetation surrounding the entrance, the city ceases to exist inside this tropical oasis and arboreal retreat.

If you are a tree lover, Foster garden is your sanctuary, a second home. And even if trees aren't your first love, you'll be taken back and amazed at the lofty enormity of many of the trees planted on the grounds. German physician and botanist William Hillebrand planted many of the living giants that dominate the garden's canopy. When Queen Kalama leased a small parcel to him and his wife in 1853,

top: The orchid garden was started with Dr. Harold Lyon's personal collection, some of which still bloom today. bottom left: Vanda orchids cling tight to hapu'u logs. bottom right: Tall and mature trees are the draw at Foster.

Hillebrand broke earth, building a house and planting trees on what is now the main terrace of the garden.

Some years later, the property was sold to Thomas and Mary Foster, who continued to add to the garden, slowly building the tropical collection. In 1930, upon Mrs. Foster's death, the 5.5-acre parcel was donated to the City and County of Honolulu as a public garden, which opened to the public on Nov. 30, 1931. Dr. Harold Lyon was the first director and used his own orchid collection to start the orchid garden, which still blooms today.

left: This earpod tree is an Exceptional Tree and grows to a height of 125 feet. Brown, ear-shaped seedpods give the tree its common name. center: The smooth buttressed trunk of the mighty kapok. The floss encased within its seedpod is waterproof and used for stuffing life preservers, pillows and mattresses. right: The magnificent inflorescence of the talipot palm, a once-in-its-lifetime occurrence.

Under the direction of Paul R. Weissich, from 1957 to 1989, the trees continued to grow as did the acreage of the garden, expanding to the present 13.5 acres. Now the canopy trees of the main terrace—the two smooth-bark kapok trees from tropical America, a giant crape myrtle from Australia, the hog plum from tropical America, and the tropical American earpod, with massive limbs and bulbous woody growths— each have trunk girths of 8 to 12 feet in diameter.

These magnificent trees, along with many others sprinkled throughout the garden, comprise 26 of Oʻahu's 100-plus "Exceptional Trees." In 1975, the Hawaiʻi State Legislature enacted a law to safeguard designated trees from injury and destruction. They deemed these trees Exceptional Trees. Designations of exceptional status are awarded to specific trees based on age, location, rarity, size, aesthetic quality, endemic status or historical and cultural significance. The number, variety and uniqueness of the exceptional trees growing in Foster Botanical Gardens is definitely one of the horticulture highlights of this garden.

Whether you drop in for a quick stroll through the garden or for a more in depth look at the plants, flowers and birds, Foster is a must see. It's a quiet place to relax, a great place to get some clean air and exercise or for an afternoon in low gear.

left: The squatty trunk of the baobab tree; very large, yet still a juvenile. center: The cannonball tree, another Exceptional Tree, is a member of the Brazilian-nut family and its heavy, round fruit grows on special stems off the trunk. right: The tattele tree is from the Brazilian Amazon and is very rapid growing tree.

A shady spot on Croton Terrace.

Once you are greeted by the stately Caribbean royal palms upon your entrance, also Exceptional Trees, walk across the Croton Terrace, following the path to your left, through the gazebo and into the bromeliad and orchid gardens. Bright color vanda orchids cling to hapu'u (Hawaiian tree fern) stumps and other epiphytic bromeliads, and orchids hang and flourish from trees and shrubs in this beautifully landscaped nook.

Past the low-lying old house, the compact orchid garden opens up to the awe-inspiring main terrace with three massive canopy trees, an earpod and two kapok trees, branches flung far and wide. From afar they resemble people dancing in the breeze, with branches for arms and buttressed trunks as legs. The kapok produces hollow, waterproof filaments in its seedpod that is used for life preservers, pillows, mattresses and upholstery.

Towards the rear of the main terrace, on the border of the palm garden is another Exceptional Tree, a tall and skinny hoop pine, native to eastern Australia. After that it's all palms. Don't miss the native Hawaiian loulu palm that is over 100 years old, or the talipot palm, with silvery fronds at least 6 feet in diameter.

The wide-open, walk-anywhere landscaping narrows to winding trails through the prehistoric glen in the center of the garden. These plants might not be as old as the trees growing in the main terrace, but their evolutionary lineage traces back in time to the Jurassic period, some 200 million years ago when gymnosperms, cone-bearing plants, dominated the landscape. Different species of cycads are close-packed throughout the glen. These interesting, rigid-leafed plants were around long before plants evolved flowers, much like ferns, and thrive in Oʻahu's warm and moist climate. Cycads are usually slow growing, but in this glen they have nearly taken over, creating a very lush spectacle as the plants arch and bend towards each other, thick blade-like leaves intermingling, large cones emerging from the center of female plants in bloom.

As you meander through the winding trail, watch out for falling cannonballs. Since cycads tend to be low lying plants, make sure to look up once in a while to keep your eyes peeled for the cannonball tree. With heavy spherical fruit growing off stems on the main trunk, cannonbals can drop when least expected. The oddity of a tree trunk covered in cannonball shaped fruit was enough to deem this specimen exceptional.

On the outskirts of the prehistoric glen is the herb garden, the economic garden with examples of spices, dyes, poisons and beverage plants. Locate the large, lone standing calabash nutmeg tree next to some offices. Walk around to the side and find another orchid surprise, the hybrid orchid showcase. This window display shows off a multitude of rare, exotic and colorful spikes full of blooms.

Spin around from the orchid display to find yourself on the Daibutsu Terrace. On your left is a tree native to tropical East Africa thought to be extinct in the wild, *Gigasiphon macrosiphon*. It has large white flowers that open early in the evenings. On the other side of the terrace is the official tree of Honolulu, the shower tree hybrid 'Wilhelmina Tenney.' Continue on past the color splash of the shower tree and into the middle terrace with heliconias, palms, gingers and a fern glade. Don't miss the foreboding, swollen and smooth-trunked quipo tree, which was planted in the 1930s.

From here you're back where you started, right by the Caribbean royal palms near the entrance.

Hālawa Xeriscape Garden

99-1268 Iwaena Street, 'Aiea, Hawai'i 96701

Contact: (808) 748-5041

Directions: From Honolulu take the H-1 West onto Route 78/Moanalua Freeway. Take the Hālawa/Stadium off-ramp, turn right at the first light and left onto 'Iwa'iwa Street, then take the first right onto Iwaena Street. Drive to the end, approx. 1 mile, and enter the Hālawa Xeriscape Garden driveway. Follow the road past the visitor center and shaded parking is on the left.

Hours Daily: Saturday from 9:00 a.m. to 3:00 p.m.

Closed: Monday thru Friday and Sunday

Admission: Free

Guided Hikes: By appointment at (808) 748-5041.

Facilities: Restrooms, drinking fountains, picnic area, outdoor covered demonstration area.

Not a problem

~50 inches

3 acres

Water thrifty plants

165 feet

Level stone and cement paths with gradual inclines

Slippers

The Hālawa Xeriscape Garden may not be a green tropical garden, but it does serve a very useful and necessary purpose as a xeriscape demonstration garden. Xeriscape is a gardening concept that employs water-thrifty plants and other water saving techniques to conserve water outdoors. When someone mentions xeriscape, what immediately follows is the stereotype of a garden full of rocks and cacti, but the Honolulu Board of Water Supply's Xeriscape Garden hopes to shatter this myth with their beautiful potpourri of water-thrifty native and exotic species, and a visual example of how it can be done.

Opened to the public in 1989, the three-acre garden boasts nearly 200 different varieties of water thrifty plants found throughout the dryland tropics of the world. In addition, much care has

top left: The visitor center and workshop in the background. top right: Loulu palms thrive in the dry climate of Hālawa Valley. bottom: A mature monkeypod tree offers a nice place to lay down a blanket and snooze in the shade.

been taken to bolster the garden's collection of native Hawaiian plant species adapted to hot and dry conditions.

When the goal is less water usage in the garden, several conditions are a must: good soil, mulch and plants that thrive in hot and drier climates. You'll notice immediately that most of the garden floor is covered in ground covers or mulch. Either way, the purpose is to prevent the loss of water through evaporation and with organic mulches, there is the added benefit of nutrients returning to the soil. Yes, the garden does contain succulents, but there are also numerous examples of trees, native palms, herbs and shrubs that love less water.

The garden is situated on a gently-sloping hillside and most of the collection is planted in the sun on the upper portion of the slope. A level stone and cement path winds through the plantings of native Hawaiian species, international drought tolerant plants, a bromeliad garden and tree garden. Flowers bloom and green leaves soak up the sun, so if you're thinking about a water-saving change in your garden, take a close look at the plants used and the methods in which they are arranged.

Towards the bottom of the property massive monkeypod, earpod, royal Poinciana and kukui trees shade a large grassy area, offering up a cool spot to get out of the sun and the heat. It's relatively quiet, save for the constant white noise of the H-3, which is out of sight, but not out of earshot.

If you are considering planting a water-wise garden, the Hālawa Xeriscape garden holds frequent workshops in their shaded outdoor classroom. In addition, knowledgeable staff are on hand for tours of the garden, but by appointment only. Whether redesigning the front yard or just getting ideas for a future project, this garden definitely serves its purpose.

Mulch and drought-tolerant ground cover plants keep the soil cooler and reduce surface water evaporation.

Ho'omaluhia Botanical Garden
(Honolulu Botanical Gardens)

45-680 Luluku Rd., Kāne'ohe, Hawai'i 96744

Contact: (808) 233-7323, www.co.honolulu.hi.us/parks/hbg/hmbg.htm

Directions: From the Likelike Highway (63) heading east, turn right on Anoi Road, turn right on Luluku Road.

Hours Daily: 9:00 a.m. to 4:00 p.m.

Closed: Christmas Day and New Year's Day

Admission: Free

Guided Hikes: Free. Saturday at 10 a.m. and Sundays at 1 p.m. Call to register. Groups up to 60 people welcome with reservations. Hike is 2 to 3 hours long.

Facilities: Information/visitor center, lecture hall, workshop, exhibition room, restrooms.

Fishing: Free. Catch and release only. Saturday and Sunday from 10 a.m. to 2 p.m. Contact visitor center for reservations and permits.

Camping: Free from 9 a.m. Friday to 4 p.m. Monday. Check in with visitor center for camping and parking permits.

Be prepared, they're hungry

100 inches

400 acres

Lake Waimaluhia and rustic campground

~260 feet

Mud, gravel, dirt, grass, asphalt, hills

Shoes

Ho'omaluhia Botanical Garden is a natural embodiment of its translation, "a place of peace and tranquility." However, before its inception some 25 years ago, this was hardly the case. In 1965 and 1969, torrential floodwaters ran down the valley and inundated the residential neighborhood of Keapuka, turning the quiet area into a wreckage of mud and debris. Two people lost their lives in the natural disaster.

To curb the destructive force of any further flooding, the Army Corps of Engineers designed and built a dam across Kamo'oali'i Stream. Construction began in 1976 and was finished in 1980. Soon after a new lake emerged that averages 10 feet deep and covers 37 acres.

top: Lake Waimaluhia. bottom left: Lake Waimaluhia and the Koʻolau Mountains. bottom right: Sealing wax palm.

The dam is made mostly of earthfill, material taken from the digging of the reservoir. An intake tower in the lake keeps an even flow of water moving through a conduit under the dam and into the Kamoʻoaliʻi Stream. Floodwaters use this same exit and in case of that "100-year storm," a spillway is prepared to handle excess flow. It would take a monumental amount of rain to make use of that spillway, as the dam is constructed to hold back water up to 57 feet deep, which would expand the lake to 152 acres momentarily.

In 1982, the botanical garden opened its gates to the public. Nestled snugly at the base of the verdant and dramatic corduroy cliffs of the Koʻolau Mountains in

Kāneʻohe, the garden boasts 400 acres of endangered and rare plants from eight tropical regions of the world. These separate planting—Malaysian, Tropical American, India/Sri Lanka, Melanesian, Native Hawaiian, Polynesian, African, Hau Trees—are spread across the garden, linked by a curvy paved road, each section with its own small parking lot and trail system. With over 10,000 plants from the tropics, there is a lot to see.

Hoʻomaluhia Botanical Garden contains an amazing collection of palms, but be prepared for the occasional rainsquall passing through.

The main gate opens and closes promptly at 9:00 a.m. and 4:00 p.m., respectively. If you come earlier or later, you can walk into the garden through a pedestrian entrance in the gate. There are a few undesignated spots on the side of the road next to the entrance where you can park your vehicle.

As you walk, or drive, up the palm fringed and hilly main road, the first geographical planting you'll happen upon are the Philippine plants on your left. Once you pass over the Kuou Stream, the garden morphs into Malaysian plants. Up ahead is a compound of low-lying buildings and a parking lot. This is the maintenance area and visitor center.

The visitor center at Hoʻomaluhia Botanical Garden is something you don't want to miss. There's always something going on inside that adds to the experience of the gardens. They have a lecture room and workshop where various

left: Typhonodorum sp. *from Madagascar. right: The curious flower of the lipstick plant,* Bixa orellana.

classes, community events and botanical workshops are held. An exhibition hall displays art and other botanically related pieces. They have a botanical library, a great resource, and the visitor center itself is a mini museum, focusing on flora and fauna, Hawaiian ethnobotany and the history of the park. It is staffed with knowledgeable and friendly experts who can answer your botanical questions as well as set you up with permits for fishing, camping, overnight vehicles and information on up coming events. Ho'omaluhia is a big, spread-out garden, so grab a map and start exploring.

Just behind the visitor center a vast clearing guides you down to the lake's edge.

While you're checking out the visitor center, don't miss the courtyard in between the visitor center, the workshop and the exhibition hall, which features the 24 canoe plants of ancient Hawai'i, brought over by Polynesian travels aboard their canoes.

The Tropical American planting is located just beyond the visitor center and trees and shrubs pepper the path to the lake. Huge canopy trees shade a big grassy lawn, great for protection from the sun or intermittent rainsquall. The

Tropical American planting is very accessible from the parking lot and has a day-use area for picnicking.

There are several trails that break off from the Tropical Americas planting, two of which are lake trails. One heads north, through the Malaysian and Philippine plants and once it crosses over the Kuou stream, it skirts the bank of the lake to the foot of the flood-control dam and the fishing area. The other lake trail heads south through the Tropical American planting. Once you cross the first bridge, turn right to go to the India/Sri Lanka planting, or stay left to continue on the lake trail. The trail bends and curves with the contours of the lake and connects to the Native Hawaiian planting. Another trail originating in the Tropical American planting delivers you into the neighboring India/Sri Lanka planting.

The Native Hawaiian section has a self-guided hike identifying 18 endemic and indigenous Hawaiian plants along the trail. Make sure to pick up a special brochure for Kahua Lehua, the Native Hawaiian planting, in the visitor center. It has a map of the loop trail and a detailed description of the 18 identified plants marked along the path.

Another great way to view the individual geographic planting is simply to drive to the planting of your choice, park and stroll through the trees, shrubs and flowering plants of the represented region. Once you get away from the visitor center or off the main road, the natural landscape is in command, so come prepared for dirt paths and trails with exposed roots, leaf litter, and the occasional mud bog.

Unique to Hoʻomaluhia is Lake Waimaluhia, meaning peaceful fresh water, and its shoreline fishing program. Catch and release fishing is permitted from the banks of the lake at the foot of the flood-control dam on Saturdays and Sundays from 10:00 a.m. to 2:00 p.m. It's a beautiful 20-minute walk to the shoreline and there are no facilities, so make sure to bring water, snacks and only the necessities.

Due to the garden's size and its function as a natural preserve, Hoʻomaluhia is able to offer rustic camping on the weekends. Tent camping is by permit only from 9:00 a.m. Friday through 4:00 p.m. Monday. Permits are available at the visitor center throughout the week. The facilities include restrooms and cold-water showers, you'll need to bring the rest: hibachi, lantern, tent, cooler, etc. The Koʻolau Mountains receive around 100 inches of rain a year, so be prepared for everything from an afternoon sprinkle to an all-day downpour.

Kapi'olani Community College Cactus Garden

4303 Diamond Head Road, Honolulu, Hawai'i, 96816

Contact: None

Directions: From H-1 East exit King Street, turn right onto Kapahulu Avenue, turn left on Paki Avenue, turn left on Monsarrat Avenue, Monsarrat Avenue becomes Diamond Head Road. KCC is on the left. Turn left right before the white chapel and park in Lot C off Diamond Head Road.

Hours Daily: Sunrise to Sunset

Admission: Free

Guided Hikes: Not offered

Facilities: Benches

Nope

Less than 25 inches

Less than 1 acre

Thorns

~187 feet

Inclined paved paths and uneven gravel

Either

If you like succulents, then at the KCC Cactus Garden you'll feel like a kid in a candy store. The thorny and well-kept garden of cacti and succulents borders the 'Ilima (administration) Building's southeast flank, facing Diamond Head, and is chock full of water thrifty plants from around the world. From the fine needles of the hairy old man to the multicolored flowers and bulbous caudex of the desert rose, the garden naturally sprouts out of the rocky slope.

Created by student and volunteer Moriso Teraoka in the late 1980s, the landscaped hillside is now a hallmark of KCC's campus. The impressive assortment of succulents was donated by members of the Cactus and Succulent Society of Hawai'i and strategically planted on Teraoka's accord. Fleshy green arms covered in thorns reach up to the sky just as other low-lying species, like agave, fill in the nooks and crannies below the waist.

From the sidewalk, a path snakes up the hillside, dissecting the garden. There are several benches along the path and places where you can enter the succulent refuge and get an up-close-and-personal look at many of the unique plants. Keep your hands to yourself and walk slowly and carefully on the mulched pathways. The trails are uneven, rocks and boulders abound and spiny arms of cacti reach all around. If you're snapping photos and need to adjust your frame of reference, make sure you look behind yourself before backing up. Otherwise you could be taking home some unwanted souvenirs.

The garden is best viewed on the weekends, when parking is free (there is no permit required) and campus life slows to a crawl. The quiet is consoling and the Diamond Head backdrop with the midday sun will invoke the sensation of wandering through the desert.

left: The small garden is seamlessly designed with rocks, plants and paths married in a natural setting. right: Look, but don't touch.

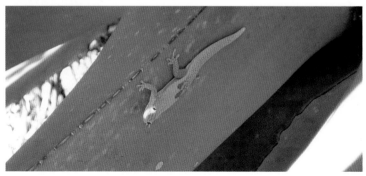

A day gecko scurries across a broad agave leaf.

top: It's not often one finds barrel cactus growing in Hawai'i. bottom left: desert rose. bottom right: You can walk through the cactus garden, just keep an eye out for a thorny cactus arm.

Koko Crater Botanical Garden
(Honolulu Botanical Gardens)

At the end of Kokonani Street, inside Koko Crater, adjacent to the Koko Crater Stables.

Contact: (808) 522-7063, www.co.honolulu.hi.us/parks/hbg/kcbg.htm

Directions: Take H-1 East till it becomes HI-72, pass Sandy Beach Park and turn left onto Kealahou Street, turn left onto Kokonani Street.

Hours Daily: Sunrise to Sunset

Closed: Christmas Day and New Year's Day

Admission: Free

Guided Hikes: Free. Guided group tours may be arranged by appointment. The hike is 2 hours long.

Facilities: No restrooms, drinking water or visitor center. Please use facilities at nearby Sandy Beach.

- You're in the clear
- 12 to 20 inches
- 60 acres
- Plumeria cultivars
- Just above sea level
- Rocks, sand, dirt and gravel
- Shoes

Koko Crater Botanical Garden, on the southeastern tip of the island, is located inside Koko Crater, adjacent to the Koko Crater Stables. Just as its name implies, Koko Crater is a cinder cone remaining from the last active volcano on Oʻahu, which erupted roughly 10,000 to 50,000 years ago. It is also the tallest tuff ring in Hawaiʻi as well, the ridgeline rising 1,207 ft. from sea level.

What is a tuff ring? It's a wide, low-rimmed, well-bedded accumulation of hyalo-clastic debris built around a volcanic vent. In other words, it's the well-known sloping conical shape of volcanoes in this region.

The crater, formed around two closely associated vents, is actually a combination of two sister craters that interconnect to give the impression of one large crater. A smaller outer crater, the site of the fragrant hybrid plumeria grove and the entrance to the gardens, narrows and then opens up to the much larger

Koko Crater Botanical Garden is actually inside the crater, its walls standing guard all around the arid garden.

and expansive inner crater, whose succulent covered inner walls rise formidably to the sky.

The ancient Hawaiians incorporated Koko Crater into their story and lore of Pele, the volcano goddess. During Pele's stay in Kalapana, on the island of Hawai'i, she was attacked by Kamapua'a, the pig god. In order to protect Pele, her sister, Kapo, distracted Kamapua'a by luring him to O'ahu. Being a lecherous and lascivious god, Kamapua'a followed Kapo's lure, her vagina (kohe), to the spot where it came to rest on a hill, forming an impression known to the ancient Hawaiians as kohe-lepelepe, and known today as Koko Crater.

In 1958, Koko Crater was transformed from barren cattle pastures into a botanical garden. Of the 200 acres inside the crater, 60 acres of the inner slope were cultivated with rare and endangered dryland plants, accustomed to the natural desert-like surroundings inside the crater. All the botanicals are water thrifty, conserving water in their leaves, stems or in tubers under the ground. With only 12 to 20 inches of rain a year, Koko Crater is the cornerstone of the Honolulu Botanical Garden's dryland plant collection.

The two-mile loop trail begins in the outer crater with the hybrid plumeria grove and bougainvillea cultivars, then horseshoes through four major collections arranged geographically throughout the inner crater: the Americas, Native Hawaiian plants, Madagascar, Africa, and an extensive collection of dryland palms from around the world.

Kiawe, or mesquite trees, and koa haole are abundant throughout the crater and along the hike, introduced as fodder for the grazing cattle. Native pili grass, thought to originally line the crater walls, is no longer found.

One of the major draws of this garden, the plumeria grove, was planted in the 1960s, a collaboration of two authorities on plumeria propagation and hybridization, Jim Little and Donald Angus. Long and gangly, fleshly branches reach fifteen feet up into the air, only to droop and sag to the ground, forming a web-like network of sap filled trusses supporting a canopy of newly emerging bright green leaves and tufts of flowers. This plumeria grove is the largest collection in one area. The mature grove is planted from light color flowers, the pin-wheeled whites and pinks with sweet scents, in the front, to the darkest flowers, crimson and blood red with spicy, gingery fragrance, in the back. These deciduous trees lose their leaves and flowers and enter a period of dormancy from early winter to early spring. In March and April, bouquets of colorful flowers begin to bloom and waxy green leaves emerge from nubby, fleshy branches. By May, the inflorescences are in full bloom and the whole crater is perfumed by the display.

The dirt trail surrounding the stand of plumeria is flanked by brightly colored bougainvillea cultivars on the lower crater wall with long, arching arms of leaves and flowers reaching for the sun, leading you to the next planting. Keep your hands to yourself in the Americas section as the trail is lined, and sometimes invaded, by a variety of cacti from the American continent. Thorns are the draw

left and right: Beginning in March, brilliant displays of color and fragrance emerge from dormant plumeria branches. The silky flowers come in many forms and colors.

here, with spiky appendages protruding from the round golden barrel cactus, the hairy and gangly old man cactus, agave, yucca, blue cactus and the pereskia tree, harboring both leaves and thorns to ward off predators from its golden fruit. The jatropha tree (*Jatropha curcas*) is also featured. Its oil being widely accepted as a form of biodeisel.

Cacti give way to an array of cycads from Mexico on the way to the remnants of a massive wiliwili (*Erythrina sandwicensis*) grove that once stretched from Koko Crater to Sandy Beach. With costly painstaking efforts, Koko Crater Botanical

top left: An ominous entrance to the Americas section. top right: The plumeria grove is planted from light colors in the front, morphing to deep hues of red and purple in the back. bottom: Mesquite trees are the dominant trees of the inner-crater landscape.

Garden was able to save much of its small wiliwili grove inside the crater from the invasive and deadly gull wasp with pesticides injected into the trunks of the native trees. The native Hawaiian plant section of the garden features the endangered loulu palm, its leaves used for thatch, native hibiscus, and the alahe'e tree. The ancient Hawaiians would burn the wood of the alahe'e and use the charcoal to make dye for tattoos.

Duck under the hanging woody fruit of the sausage tree in the Madagascar section and look for *Alluaudia procera*. The spiny tree is home to lemurs in its native setting. The trail continues into the Africa planting. Marvel at the swollen bulbous trunks of the baobab tree, also known as the dead rat tree because of its conspicuous fury fruit, which resembles a dead rat hanging by its tail. Also planted in the area are henna tree, popular for a reddish-brown dye made from the seeds, aromatic frankincense, African gardenias and desert rose.

As the trail rounds out the larger inner crater, it deposits you back into the plumeria garden of the outer crater for one last stroll through the magnificent array of plumeria cultivars. A tangible example of aloha.

left: A thorny planting all around. right: Many different species of cycads from the Americas thrive in the garden.

Leeward Community College Hawaiian Botanical Collection

96-045 Ala Ike, Pearl City, Hawai'i 96782

Contact: (808) 455-0251

Directions: From H-1 West, take the Waipahu exit 8B. Stay in the left lane and make a U-turn at the first light by Waipahu High School. Look for the LCC sign and follow the sign over the freeway. Take a right and the parking lots are on the left.

Hours Daily: 8:00 a.m. to 4:00 p.m.

Closed: Weekends and holidays

Admission: Free

Guided Hikes: Schedule a guided tour of the collection through the math and science department at (808) 455-0251.

Facilities: Restrooms and drinking water available across campus.

Nope, you're in the clear

Less than 20 inches

Spread throughout the 49 acre campus

Native Hawaiian dryland species

50 to 70 feet

Paved roads and walkways

Either would do the trick

While it may not be the easiest garden to find on the island, it is one of the last bastions for many rare or endangered dryland native Hawaiian plant species growing in the Wai'anae Mountains and other locales across the islands. With over 130 endemic and indigenous plants, 35 of which are endangered, thriving in manicured plantings across the campus, the LCC Hawaiian Botanical Collection is an opportunity for the public to see rare and endangered plants that only trained field botanists will have the opportunity to see in the wild.

Bruce Koebele, author, former LCC instructor and authority on Hawai'i plant propagation, planted most of the campus' mature native trees in the collection. He started the garden in the mid 1990s. Designed to educate as well as to engage students and the public in native plant conservation and propagation, about half of the plants were started from

left: *Endangered alula grow in the LCC Shade House.* right: *The grape-like fruit of the Kauaian endemic* Munroidendron racemosum *leaves a red-wine stain when smashed.*

wild collected seeds given to the garden by conservationist collectors holding the proper permits in an effort to bolster populations of extremely rare Hawaiian dryland species.

The best way to view the garden and get the whole scoop about the individual plants and their uses in Hawaiian culture is to set up an appointment to tour the collection. Tag along with faculty and staff from the botany department, or possibly luck out and score a ride in the Collection Manager's golf cart around the garden.

The 45-minute tour kicks off at the Shade House, an academic propagation center where students learn the groundwork for propagation and conservation in this outdoor shaded facility. Students learn to propagate plants to be used in the collection or for their annual plant sale. They also propagate plants for use in restoration projects, like growing koa for a Mākaha burn site restoration.

The tour snakes up the hillside past the Shade House, where endangered 'ōhai from Ka'ena Point, a low lying shrub with far-reaching branches and small, orchid-like peach flowers hiding beneath silver foliage, joins other endangered plants from O'ahu. Other prime specimens are three mature Big Island kauila trees, 'uhi'uhi, of which there are only a handful of individual trees left in the Wai'anae Mountains and the curiously prehistoric and endangered *Munroidendron racemosum* from Kaua'i, with simple alternating branch structure and long dangling clusters of purple and yellow flowers that become soft and round

left: The Stream Garden gives beauty to a campus courtyard. right: Sugarcane and sweet potato in the ethnobotanical garden.

marble-sized fruits that leave a rich, port-wine stain when squashed. Underneath the tree, the native ground cover 'akulikuli spreads out evenly with turgid fleshy stalks pointing skyward.

The LCC native collection is proud to line their paths with native pili grass, something not found at most botanical gardens. The bushy clumps of thick grass seem to have dark clumps of dead grass stuck towards the ends of the stalks. Upon closer inspection, the clumps are actually tangled and fibrous seed masses, which fall to the ground and untangle with each subsequent rain. The corkscrew-shaped seed and follicle screws itself into the soil where it remains dormant for six months before emerging to grace the landscape.

The botanical garden, which is organically managed, is not all natives, and of course, they include a garden of plants with ethnobotanical uses. Polynesian introduced medicinal and food plants are found alongside plants with special organic uses, like tobacco, which is used to brew a natural pesticide.

Clutched in between two rows of classrooms is the Stream Garden, where loulu palms and a yellow-flowered ōhi'a lehua tree stand tall over a small mean-dering stream filled with koi fish and lined with native ferns. Next to the Stream Garden is the Ōhi'a Garden, planted with several ōhi'a lehua trees with different types of leaves, some lobed and round, others curly or wavy, yet all the seeds were collected from Big Island lava fields. The ōhi'a lehua garden is the perfect demonstration alluding to the native tree's scientific name, *Metrosideros polymorpha*, meaning many forms. The ōhi'a tree is one species of tree, yet its flowers vary in color and leaves vary in form.

Up by the parking lot is a planting called Clay's Garden, a memorial garden for Horace Clay, which is filled with the delicate, red-flowering Clay's hibiscus, or koki'o 'ula, a native endemic hibiscus. It's a beautiful send off from this garden of native rarities.

top: Curly leaf ōhi'a lehua trees with yellow blossoms and loulu palm in the Ōhi'a Garden. bottom left: The simple structure of Munroidendron racemosum. *bottom right: A seed mass clinging to the blades of native pili grass waits for a rain to break it apart and drive it into the ground.*

Lili'uokalani Botanical Garden
(Honolulu Botanical Gardens)

N. Kuakini Street, Honolulu, Hawai'i 96817

Contact: (808) 522-7060, www.co.honolulu.hi.us/parks/hbg/

Directions: Parking lot on N. Kuakini Street between Nu'uanu Avenue and Huli Street.

Hours Daily: 7:00 a.m. to 5:00 p.m.

Closed: Christmas Day and New Year's Day

Admission: Free

Guided Hikes: Not available

Facilities: Restrooms

Where there's water, there are mosquitoes

30 to 40 inches

7.5 acres

45 to 60 feet

Sloped cement path

Slippers

The smallest of the Honolulu Botanical Gardens, Lili'uokalani Botanical Garden was once the property and favorite picnic grounds of Queen Lili'uokalani, Hawai'i's last reigning monarch. The garden is devoted to native Hawaiian plants and features the gurgling waters of Nu'uanu Stream and gentle Waikahalulu Waterfall towards the southern end of the garden.

Lili'uokalani Botanical Garden seems more like a neighborhood park than a botanical garden. Flanked by a high-rise apartment building and busy Nu'uanu Ave. on the east side of the stream. The stream and waterfall are a nice distraction from the hustle and bustle of Honolulu, that is, if you can block out the hanging laundry and cluttered balconies of the apartment building.

Most of the Hawaiian plants are arranged along the cement path, which meanders down the slight grade of the rectangular parcel of land. Placards identify Hawaiian and scientific names along the trail. Shade-giving monkeypod canopy trees line the banks of the stream and there is a flat grassy area by the waterfall. It's not a good idea to swim or wade in the stream, as it is prone to run off water. In addition, do not leave any valuables in your car in plain sight.

Nu'uanu Stream meanders through rocks and boulders under a canopy of monkeypod trees.

Harold L. Lyon Arboretum

3860 Mānoa Road, Honolulu, Hawaiʻi 96822

Contact: (808) 988-0456 www.hawaii.edu/lyonarboretum

Directions: From the H-1, exit University Avenue and head mauka (toward the mountains). University Avenue becomes Oahu Avenue. Follow Mānoa Road up the valley and turn left into the Arboretum's driveway at the end of Mānoa Road. Parking is located by the visitor center.

Hours Daily: Monday – Friday from 8:00 a.m. to 4:00 p.m., Saturday from 9:00 a.m. to 3:00 p.m.

Closed: Sunday and state holidays

Admission: Suggested donation of $5 per person

Guided Hikes: Guided Tours are available daily from 10 a.m. to 11:30 a.m., $5 per person. Call (808) 988-0461 in advance for scheduling and to reserve a space.

Facilities: Visitor center, book store, gift shop, restrooms, drinking fountains, and plants are for sale at the main greenhouse.

 Oh yeah! Insect repellent is a must

 165 inches

193.5 acres

Verdant Mānoa Valley

450 to 1850 feet

 Cobble stone paths with gravel and grass, gravel and flagstone paths, dirt forest and cliff trails for experienced hikers. Paths may be uneven due to protruding roots, rocks or erosion.

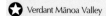 Shoes

Standing at the visitor center, looking across a sea of dense green foliage nestled up against the cloud-cloaked pali, it's hard to image that as late as 1918, the landscape was nearly devoid of vegetation, save for grasses and thickets of weeds. The demise of the natural vegetation was not the act of a terrible flood or by the hand of man, it was primarily caused by voracious free-ranging cattle.

In 1918, the Hawaiian Sugar Planter's Association (HSPA) purchased 124 acres of land in the upper Mānoa valley to establish a research station to demonstrate the value of watershed restoration, test tree species for use in restoration efforts throughout Hawaiʻi and to collect plants of economic value. They brought in plant pathologist Dr. Harold L. Lyon, who was also placed in charge of the Department of Botany and Forestry for the Territory of Hawaiʻi, to

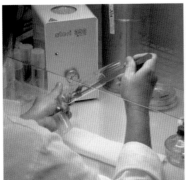

left: Conservation and perpetuation of native species is of paramount importance at Lyon Arboretum. A volunteer cares for a young, propagated rare native plant. right: The micro-propagation lab, where rare native plants are raised for future outplanting efforts.

left: Detailed records are kept of the lineage of the plant and its care while in the facility. right: Once a suitable site is ready, the delicate rare plants are grown up in a nursery on the premises.

re-forest the barren landscape. Native trees would not grow on the trampled earth and earlier attempts to plant ironwood, eucalyptus and silver oak failed to retain rain run-off for water conservation, so Dr. Lyon brought in thousands of species of exotic trees, vines and shrubs. For nearly thirty years he experimented with many different introduced species and finally accomplished his goal.

Sugarcane was short-lived in the valley, but the ficus and albizia trees stand tall today, comprising much of the canopy we see. In 1953 the experimental station, called Mānoa Arboretum, was passed on to the University of Hawai'i with

left: Hapu'u ferns. center: Ōhi'a lehua. right: Stand of royal palms.

the provision that the facility must remain an arboretum and botanical garden in perpetuity. When Dr. Lyon passed away in 1957, the arboretum was renamed in his honor.

Under the university's direction, the focus of the arboretum has shifted significantly from forestry to horticulture and the conservation of native Hawaiian plants. Recently, more than 2,000 ornamental and economical plants have been introduced to the arboretum, with a focus on native Hawaiian and Polynesian introduced plants. A seed bank for seed storage and a plant micropropagation lab has been established to rescue rare and endangered native Hawaiian plant species from extinction and bolster numbers for re-establishment back into the wild.

Lyon Arboretum provides a unique experience for plant enthusiasts as well as hikers and botanical explorers. The trees and plants along the main road and most accessible trails offer a variety of botanicals to immerse yourself in, from native Hawaiian plants and the Hawaiian Ethnobotany Garden, to the massive trunks of canopy trees feathered with clinging aroids and curious blooms of leafy heliconia. But botanical rewards await for the adventurous and sure-footed hiker that is willing to venture off the main road and hike the network of paths and trails that snake through the 10 valleys comprising the 'Aihualama watershed.

Sign in at the visitor's center and let the fun begin. The grounds around the center are planted with herbs and spice trees from around the world with manicured plantings separated by region including European, African, Mediterranean, Asian, Chinese, New World and Gingers and Edible Flowers. A quiet pavilion with pond and lotus fountain affords a tranquil getaway for those with limited time or unaccustomed to the rocky, muddy main path through the arboretum.

Just beyond the visitor center the Hawaiian Ethnobotanic Garden sweeps downhill, providing colorful examples of plants traditionally used in Hawaiian culture. This is one of the largest collections of ethnobotanicals, Polynesian introductions and their native variations that flourish today, all surrounded by native ferns and 'ōhi'a lehua trees among others. The 'awa (kava) collection is one of the largest of its kind, representing all the known Hawaiian varieties.

Pick up the main road by walking across the lawn and slightly uphill or follow the path just below the large banyon tree. The main road and auxiliary trails are marked with wooden posts with numbers and letters that correspond to the trail map. For instance, as you embark on the main road from the parking lot, look for marker 1A on your left. Follow that trail to an open-air rain structure and a statue of Buddha next to a bo tree. Several trails snake through Fern Valley and the Bromeliad Garden and terminate at Inspiration Point, a lawn area that overlooks parts of Mānoa.

Trekking through the valleys of Lyon Arboretum is like stepping into a rainforest arboreal world, far away from the likes of civilization. Dainty ferns, ginger, heliconia, fallen branches and the knotty and buttressed trunks of albizia trees

left: Trail or dry riverbed? This trail leads to 'Aihualama Falls. right: The main road is much easier to navigate, even though it can be muddy at times.

are your companions in the understory. Continue on the faint trails to the stately plantings of royal palms standing guard on a ridge. The towering beauties have smooth gray trunks and are planted together to form a cathedral canopy of flittering fronds.

The main road is lined with heliconia, of which the arboretum boasts 120 species and 170 variations on those species (Lyon Arboretum is a conservation center for the Heliconia Society International), banyans, Cook pines, ginger, hibiscus, prayer plants, arrowroots and a healthy dose of palms splash the sides

top left: The small flowers of this ginger inflorescence are actually inside the waxy red bracts pictured. top right: One of nearly 120 species of heliconia in the garden. bottom: The view of the Pali and the gardens from the visitor center.

left: If the goal is attraction, than this flower is doing its job. right: Mature canopy trees and ample foliage create a verdant cathedral setting throughout the garden.

of the trail with color and variation. About halfway to 'Aihualama Falls is the Hawaiian Section at marker 2E on the left. Past that planting is the Economic Section on the right, marker 3K, where trees of economic importance like fruits, nuts, medicinals, dyes, fibers and fine woods thrive.

The real gem of Lyon Arboretum has to be the palm sections and the garden's overall accumulation of palm species. With over 650 species in more than 150 genera, it is one of the world's largest living collections of palms and rattans. Palms are found throughout the garden, but are concentrated toward the back of the garden, close to the falls. Starting around marker 4C, the arboretum has plantings of a huge variety of palms from the Americas, Asia and the Pacific. At this point the main trail narrows to a single-track all the way to the waterfall, fed by a perennial stream. The palms are growing naturally, peppered throughout the damp and mossy rainforest.

There are many trails snaking around in the area so look closely at the base of the palms and other botanicals for identification placards. Mixed in with trees, ginger, heliconia, mossy rocks and muddy paths, this rainforest would take days to explore in its entirety.

If you're planning on being adventurous, hiking boots are recommended. The arboretum's website, *www.hawaii.edu/lyonarboretum*, has very accurate maps, trail and botanical descriptions to print out and take with you. It's a big, moist rainforest ripe for exploring, so cover your bases, ask for a bird-watcher's guide, pack a lunch, bring lots of drinking water, and get lost, so to speak.

Queen Kapiolani Garden

On the corner of Monsarrat Avenue and Paki Avenue in Waikīkī

Contact: City and County of Honolulu Department of Parks and Recreation
(808) 768-3003, email: parks@honolulu.gov or www.co.honolulu.hi.us/parks

Directions: From H-1 East exit King Street, turn right onto Kapahulu Avenue, turn left on Paki Avenue, turn left on Monsarrat Avenue, turn left of Leahi Avenue, the parking lot is on the left.

Hours Daily: Dawn to dusk

Admission: Free

Guided Hikes: Not offered

Facilities: Shaded picnic tables and benches, restrooms.

Not Likely

Less than 25 inches

Less than an acre

Hibiscus cultivars

Sea Level

Flat

Slippers

A beautiful, colorful and compact neighbor to the grassy and open-spaced Kapiolani Park, Queen Kapiolani Garden is a nook of calm set beside its heavily trafficked big sister across the street. Open since 1972, Queen Kapiolani Garden is easy to miss, tucked away on the corner of a busy intersection and shaded by the far-reaching canopy of the monkeypod trees lining Monsarrat Avenue.

The draw to this garden is definitely the plethora of hibiscus cultivars: the bright red and yellow contrast of the Concord; the splash of fuchsia on white petals of the King Kalakaua; the ruffley peach and red-veined Waikīkī Sand; the deep red petals with splashes of yellow of the Maroon Star; and hundreds of dainty white flowers from Hawai'i's native white hibiscus. Paved pathways divide neatly planted beds of many different cultivars, blooming throughout the year. The beds are dispersed all around the garden, which means that there are almost always hibiscus flowers showing off their colors, ruffles and ridges somewhere in the small garden.

While hibiscus might be the draw, there are many other flowerbeds planted with other beautiful botanicals. Wander across tzhe perimeter to find a bed of bougainvillea cultivars, a ti garden, tropical ornamentals and a small collection of native Hawaiian plants. In the center of the garden, beset by grassy sunlit open space, is a water-thrifty bed planted with cycads, palms and other dryland species.

top left and right: Hibiscus cultivars. bottom: Diamond Head in the distance.

Sprawling lawn connects separate plantings of unusual hibiscus cultivars and other tropical trees and ornamentals.

Native white hibiscus koki'o ke'oke'o.

The garden is full sun in the afternoon until evening, when the sun dips behind the monkeypod trees. Other than that, a noni tree and a few palms provide little shade while meandering around the garden. There is, however, a shady respite from the overhead rays under the wooden latticed shade covering near the parking lot. Several picnic tables and a few benches make this a wonderful place to enjoy a snack or have a quiet game of chess or checkers.

Senator Fong's Plantation and Gardens

47-285 Pulama Road, Kāne'ohe, Hawai'i 96744

Contact: (808) 239-6775 www.fonggarden.com info@fonggarden.com

Directions: From Honolulu, take the H-1 to Route 63, the Likelike Highway, to the 83 Kahekili Highway off ramp. Heading north, pass the Hygienic Store and keep an eye out for Pulama Road, turn left and drive up the hill.

Hours Daily: 10:00 a.m. to 2:00 p.m.

Closed: Christmas Day and New Year's Day

Admission: Adults $14.50, children $9, lei making $6.50, Special rates: Kama 'āina, school excursions, senior citizen clubs. Cash or traveler's cheques only, no credit cards.

Guided Hikes: Guided walking tours daily at 10:30 a.m. and 1 p.m.

Facilities: Restrooms, gift shop, visitor center.

Weddings: Luncheons, parties, weddings and receptions by reservation.

Yes, bring the bug spray

70 inches

725 acres

Delicious Fruit

80 to 360 feet above sea level

Hard-packed dirt road and hills

Shoes

Senator Fong's Plantation and Gardens is a 725-acre labor of love and private estate of the late Senator Hiram Leong Fong, the first U.S. Senator of Hawai'i from 1959 to 1977. Looking for a small piece of property to keep the family horses, Fong, at the time serving in Hawai'i's House of Representatives, purchased 100 acres at the base of the Ko'olau Mountains among Kahalu'u's pineapple fields in 1950, at the request of Mrs. Fong. Soon he was making use of his green thumb and turned the pineapple fields into a banana plantation that serviced the local markets.

As the surrounding land came up for sale, Fong purchases another 100-acre plot and then 500 additional acres for conservation and preservation of the natural state of the Ko'olau Mountains. The undulating landscape of his purchase was crisscrossed with dirt roads from the old pineapple plantation, so he

Cook pines leading to the Ko'olau Mountains.

left: Lychee Meadow in Kennedy Valley, one of the tastier stops along the tour. right: A staple crop at Senator Fong's Plantation and Gardens, lychee.

started planting alongside the roads to spruce up the property. His plantings of fruit trees, Cook pines, tropical botanicals, palms and other exotic trees and shrubs thrived in the moist location just off Kāne'ohe Bay and he became so fond of his gardens he opened the plantation to the public in 1988 to share his creation. Senator Fong divided his plantation into five sections and named them in honor of the presidents he served during his 17 years in the U.S. Senate: Eisenhower Plateau, Johnson Plateau, Kennedy Valley, Nixon Valley and Ford Plateau.

The botanical garden is still an operating plantation, with 200 acres dedicated to fruit and flower production. The focus on the seasonal fruit is reflected in the guided tour, so you can expect to be tasting, touching, smelling and seeing a bounty of fruits and flowers.

The one-mile, one-and-a-half hour guided walking tour commences twice daily from Eisenhower Plateau at about an 80-foot elevation. Once you leave the open-air visitor center, your senses are immediately bombarded with the smell of flowers both living and littering the ground, large orchid-like flowers consuming the spaces between the leaves of the Hong Kong orchid tree. Ornamental bananas with lilac flowers and the pale yellow whiskbroom flower of the Chinese chestnut capture the eye.

As the tour continues through Kennedy Valley, the roadside is planted with macadamia nut trees, breadfruit, mountain apple, pomelo, coffee, cocoa trees, vanilla bean vines and an assortment of ginger and heliconia.

top and bottom: Flowers abound throughout the garden.

An interesting staple in the garden are two tall and unique cannonball trees, given to Senator Fong many years ago by a mechanic friend, just seedlings in rusty tin cans. Today the towering deciduous trees, with thorny, tentacle-like branches growing from mid-trunk displaying large salmon and peach flowers and woody round fruit that look just like cannonballs, are the garden's Dr. Jekyll and Mr. Hyde, losing their leaves at completely opposite times of the year.

The canopy opens up to the spectacular lychee meadow, where five varieties of 55-year-old lychee trees produce fruit to be sold and tasted by the tour-goers. The tour takes a break under the broccoli-shaped trees to sample the goods. Farther up the valley, on the way to Johnson Plateau, is the umbrella tree rainforest with vines and lianas twisting and stretching from high up in the canopy to the forest floor. Beyond that is the palm garden, planted with raffia palms, red sealing wax palms, giant ivory nut palms, and betel nut palms to name a few.

Once you reach Johnson Plateau, the 360-foot elevation affords beautiful views of Kāneʻohe Bay and town. Adorning the plateau is another lychee orchard, the lei flower garden and coconut forest, with an additional planting of apple bananas. The towering pali juts up sharply behind the plateau and smaller, partial cinder cones are apparent in the landscape.

After a lingering Kodak moment and some quality time taking in the view, the tour loops back past plantings of sandalwood trees, ironwood, blue gum trees, rosewood trees, and Cook pines. The tour guides are exceptionally well-versed in the history of the property and the botanicals that it contains. There is plenty of road and terrain that the tour does not cover per say, so if you are in the mood to explore and your group is up for the challenge, don't be afraid to ask your guide to take a path less traveled.

top: Apple banana is found growing throughout Kennedy Valley and Norfolk pine stand tall along the ridgeline. bottom left: The view from Johnson Plateau overlooking the fruit orchard and Kāneʻohe Bay. Lychee, avocado and Meyer lemon are just a few of the fruits growing here. bottom right: Bougainvillea bonsai at the visitor center.

Tagami and Powell Gallery and Gardens

47-754 Lamaula Rd., Kāneʻohe, Hawaiʻi 96744

Contact: (808) 239-8146

Directions: From Honolulu, take the H-1 to Route 63, the Likelike Highway, to the 83 Kahekili Highway off ramp. Heading north, pass the Hygienic Store and keep an eye out for Wailehua Road, turn left on Wailehua Road, the road comes to a T, turn right onto Lamaula Road, look for a modest sign in front of a house up the hill on your left.

Hours Daily: Saturday – Monday, 10:00 a.m. to 4:00 p.m. by appointment only

Closed: Tuesday thru Friday and holidays

Admission: Free

Guided Hikes: Michael and Hiroshi will gladly show you around.

Facilities: Restrooms and several sitting areas.

Just a few

70 inches

1 acre

Hybridized anthuriums, daylilies and ti cultivars

~60 feet

Level cement paths and grass

Slippers

World-renowned artists Hiroshi Tagami and Michael Powell have blurred the lines between art and tropical landscaping, literally. Their one-acre garden is both art gallery and botanical garden, married seamlessly in a flowing union of color, images, flowers, fine art and trees. Located at the foot of the breathtaking and verdant Koʻolau Mountains, the gallery and gardens offers a rejuvenating visual retreat in more ways than one.

The two visionaries created the garden in the late 1960s, but it wasn't until the 1970s, when Hiroshi was given a federal permit to return to Hawaiʻi with plants he collected in Central and South America, that their garden's exotic tropical appearance really took root.

Once their exotics were established, Tagami began hybridizing his tropical American collection.

top: Art studios are interwoven among botanical plantings. bottom left: Edible day lilies. bottom right: Botanical oddities can be found around every corner.

Today, the garden has distinct plantings of daylilies, soft yellows and watercolor oranges, which bloom profusely from spring through the fall. Anthuriums make up a great deal of the ground cover under the shaded canopy towards the back of their property. From thumb-sized lavender anthuriums collected in Panama, Tagami developed a now-famous fragrant violet anthurium with a much larger flower. Under the shade of an African sausage tree, palms and other canopy trees, anthuriums of all colors mingle with calathea, heliconia, philodendrons and ferns in a lush and bountiful tropical array.

Tagami also has a penchant for tropical flowering trees and has strategically and beautifully placed African wisteria, two chaconia trees, the national tree of

top left: Plenty of room to relax, stroll and soak in the calm. top right: The beautiful flower of the course sandpaper tree. bottom left: Many types of anthuriums are planted throughout the garden. bottom right: A wonderland of tropical foliage creates a peaceful setting.

Trinidad boasting a massive triangular inflorescence, and pink, peach, white and his favorite, golden yellow tabebuia trees (golden trumpet trees) throughout the garden. Hidden away behind one of the gallery teahouses is a very rare sandpaper tree. Its thick leaves are rough and dry and have the texture of 80-grit sandpaper, in contrast to its soft hanging clumps of delicate light blue flowers. But to get a glimpse of this oddity, you'll have to ask.

Across a spread of lawn from a relaxing open-air covered patio, the garden also showcases a collection of Tagami's hybrid ti plants. The black ti from Costa Rica is an especially unusual variety.

In addition to the botanicals, two understated art galleries complete the landscaping, one resembling a Japanese teahouse with the artists' private studio humbly behind sliding paper doors. The galleries blend into the gardens, accented and juxtaposed by plants and trees, and feature oil paintings by Tagami and Powell, as well as fine art and sculpture by guest artists. The gallery and gardens are a collaboration of the creative energy and vision of two talented artists, both in the studio and in the garden.

left: Not only does the garden have interesting plants, it is concealed by a handful of unique trees. right: Mr. Tagami is fond of having people taste his day lilies.

University of Hawai'i at Mānoa

2444 Dole Street, Honolulu, Hawai'i, 96782

Contact: (808) 956-8111

Directions: From the H-1 East exit University Avenue, turn right onto University Avenue, turn right on Dole Street, turn left onto East-West Road. Visitor parking is located behind Kennedy Theater off East-West Road or in the parking structure on Dole Street.

Hours Daily: 24 hours a day

Admission: Free

Guided Hikes: Self-guided plant walk; stop by the Botany Department in St. John Hall for a detailed map.

Facilities: Restrooms and drinking fountains in every building. Coffee shops, eateries and vending machines abound.

Possibly in the evenings

40 inches

320 acres

Exotic trees and palms

~74 to 172 feet

Paved walkways, sidewalks and lawns

Take your pick

Over 560 different kinds of trees and plants have been used in landscaping the 320-acre campus since it was founded in 1907. Today, the well-nurtured and mature landscape is a veritable textbook of native and exotic flora that thrives in Hawai'i's warm tropical climate.

The sprawling campus and maze of tall buildings can be daunting for a newcomer, so the best way to explore the botanical collection is to follow the plant trail laid out in the Campus Plants brochure. Contact the botany department ahead of time and have one mailed to you or pick up a brochure from the botany department in St. John Hall once you arrive. In addition to the plant trail that maps out and gives a brief description of more than 80 interesting trees and plants on campus, the botany department has set up a campus plants website (*www.botany. hawaii.edu/Faculty/Carr/160webindex.htm*) that

left: With over 350 different types of trees and plants used to landscape the 320-acre campus, there is a beautiful flower, unique tree or botanical delight everywhere you look. right: The sausage tree is a native of tropical West Africa and thrives in our sub-tropical climate. The woody fruit is not edible.

details information on more than 300 species of plants found on campus and includes photographs for identification. If you just want to wander around and explore on your own, it's still a good idea to pick up a map of campus to orientate yourself with your surroundings.

Many of the established and interesting plants are located throughout the older sections of campus, from Bachman Hall on the campus's southwest corner, up past Sinclair Library across Campus Road, toward Hawai'i Hall along the Mall, to Hamilton Library and Henke Hall toward the East-West Center. The campus is home to 31 memorials trees and eight Exceptional Trees, many of which are marked with plaques.

The campus is a treasure trove for plant lovers, from bamboo and palms to colorful flowers and unique trunks, but there are several trees on campus that should not be missed. Near Sinclair Library you will definitely notice a rank and unmistakable odor wafting through the air. Stop and check out the skunk tree (an Exceptional Tree), whose red and yellow flowers give off the offensive stink. The seed inside the fruit can be eaten raw or roasted, but only in small quantities. Hunt around the library for the Mindanao gum, also known as the rainbow

left: Mature plumerias in full bloom near the Hawaiʻi Institute of Geophysics. right: A massive baobab, an Exceptional Tree, is a fitting neighbor for the Art Building.

eucalyptus with bright colors of green, yellow, orange, red and everything in between that come to life as the bark peels off the trunk.

Hawaiʻi Hall is surrounded by beautiful flora. There is a bo tree, the sacred tree of Buddhism, which was planted by the first graduating class in 1912. An array of palms also compliments the stately structure.

left: the arboreal mall behind Hawaiʻi Hall. right: The smooth and irregular trunk and limbs of the baobab.

top left: Palm planting near Hawai'i Hall. top right: Another Exceptional Tree, a mature cannonball tree, as seen from University Avenue. bottom: Shower trees line the center median of East-West Road.

A massive baobab tree, also known as the dead rat tree for the fury rat-shaped fruit that hangs from its limbs, stands tall above the Art Building on its western side. Its thick and robust trunk probably covers more square footage of land than most studio apartments in the area, and supports a beautiful canopy, complete with large, leafy white flowers.

Fronting the Hamilton Library is a small lawn with several twisted and knotted olive trees. Olive trees are rare on O'ahu and this group is crimped, twisted and thriving. From there, head over to Henke Hall, where a slew of the plants on the plant walk are growing. Hopefully you'll be witness to the bright golden floral display of the gold tree. When the gold tree is in bloom, the tree's canopy is aflame, densely covered in the brightest yellow flowers imaginable. The only thing more spectacular is when the trade winds pick up and topple the yellow blossoms to the ground in a snow of color.

Wahiawā Botanical Garden
(Honolulu Botanical Gardens)

1396 California Ave., Wahiawā, Hawai'i 96786

Contact: (808) 621-7321, www.co.honolulu.hi.us/parks/hbg/wbg.htm

Directions: From the H-2 Northbound, take Exit 8 toward Wahiawā. From HI-80 Northbound, turn right onto California Street, the garden and parking lot is on the left.

Hours Daily: 9:00 a.m. to 4:00 p.m.

Closed: Christmas Day and New Year's Day

Admission: Free

Guided Hikes: Free. Groups may request tours conducted by volunteer docents. Guided tours may be arranged by calling (808) 628-1190.

Facilities: Clean restrooms. Multipurpose room available for use by non-profit organizations.

Weddings: No charge. Allowed by permit. Groups limited to 30 persons and use is restricted to upper terrace.

They are huge!

52 to 80 inches

27 acres

O'ahu's tropical rainforest

875 to 1,000 feet

Cement, gravel, dirt and paved stairs

Shoes

Perched spectacularly on the edge of a ravine spanning the Kaukonahua Stream on a mid-elevation plateau and nestled between the Wai'anae and Ko'olau mountain ranges in Central O'ahu—the longest watershed in the state—the 875- to 1,000-foot elevation of Wahiawā Botanical Garden provides cool temperatures and ample moisture, an ideal climate, for this unique tropical rainforest.

Under the direction of Dr. Harold Lyon, the Hawai'i Sugar Planters Association leased the 27-acre parcel of land from the state of Hawai'i in 1920, using the site as an experimental arboretum. The trees planted here were tests for use in reforesting the watershed to improve water collection and drainage. In 1950, control of the land was given back to the City and County of Honolulu and subsequently opened as

a public botanical garden in 1957 and dubbed Oʻahu's "tropical jewel" by the City and County. Most of the trees planted in the garden date back to that era.

The main terrace of the garden is shaded from the intense tropical sun by large canopy trees including the fast growing banyan ficus, with mangled, twisted and buttressed trunks, the thorny geometry tree, and the round bulbous trunk of the Queensland kauri, its smooth bark flaking off in the shape of puzzle pieces. Sunlight only dapples

Canopy trees thrive at the higher elevation garden.

the grassy terrace and flitters on the broad leaves of ginger and delicate fern fronds that line the level and meandering pathway, leaving the upper terrace cool and crisp. Most of the pathway on the upper terrace is wheelchair accessible.

Here you'll also find allspice, Arabian coffee (brought to Hawaiʻi in 1813), the elephant-apple tree whose fruit is made into jelly and the chicle tree, its milky

left: Only dappled sunlight reaches the ferns on the limbs of large trees and nestled in the buttressed trunks on the main terrace. right: The colorful trunk of the Mindanao gum, also called the rainbow eucalyptus.

latex used to make the first chewing gum. The chicle tree's sugary brown fruit is also edible. Look for the pili nut tree as well. Its nutritious and oily seeds taste like almonds and are used in Chinese pastries.

Most of the flora in this garden is not growing in the ground, it's thriving on trunks and fastened to branches. Epiphytes, plants that grow on or attached to other plants, abound in this tropical rainforest, decorating the tree trunks and limbs with broad green foliage, colorful flowers and thousands of vines and lianas which hang down from the canopy, stretching to the cool earth below.

You might think that epiphytic plants are harmful to the trees, but in fact they are not parasitic and only use the tree as a fertile and moist place to grow. They receive water from rain, dew, and latent moisture in the air and find nutrients in the plant debris lodged in the crotches of branches, crevices and nooks in which they grow. The majority of epiphytes are found in tropical and sub-tropical rainforests as well as moist temperate forests.

Aroids (vines and lianas), bromeliads and orchids make up 70 percent of all the epiphytes in the world, while cacti, ferns and moss are other recognizable plants that fill in the blanks. All of these types of unique arboreal plants can be found in the garden.

On the upper terrace, orchids cover the massive limbs of banyan ficus, their large aerial roots designed specifically for the rapid absorption of water and nutrients from their environment. Staghorn ferns send out large leaves with finger-like appendages, much like the antlers of a moose or deer. Bromeliads join their epiphytic neighbors with their waxy leaves, which form a tight cup at the base to hold water and catch debris.

From the upper terrace, several paved trails wind down the bank of the ravine where you'll find many different types of aroids, their large fan-like leaves reaching for light and sending down a web of aerial roots from branches high up in the canopy. One type of aroid common in the garden is philodendron, a well-known plant that is often found at local nurseries, marketed as a small houseplant.

Down in the ravine, 47 feet below the upper terrace, there are several themed plantings and a winding dirt trail connecting each botanical section. Unobstructed sunlight is able to reach down into ravine and the plants growing there reflect the different environment.

A native Hawaiian plant section displays hibiscus, hapu'u tree ferns and a loulu palm grove among other native plants. The rocky and uneven trail snakes past a palm garden specializing in Melanesian palms, a collection of heliconia and fragrant ginger, an Okinawan garden and terminates at the bamboo forest. With a bit of wind, the bamboo forest comes alive with the curious sounds of the hollow bamboo bumping into each other with the swaying of their leafy tops.

Mosquitoes are plentiful at this garden and the zebra-striped pests are as big as helicopters. Proper clothing, long sleeves and pants, and insect repellent is recommended to deter the voracious predators.

top left: The trail leading from the main terrace into the valley. top right: Staghorn ferns are a common sight in this garden. bottom: Vines and lianas hang gingerly from branches and swing in the breeze.

Waimea Valley

59-864 Kamehameha Highway, Hale'iwa, Hawai'i 96712

Contact: (808) 638-7766

Directions: From Honolulu, take the H-1 West to the H-2 North to Kamehameha Highway heading north. Located in Waimea Valley across from Waimea Beach Park on the North Shore.

Hours Daily: 9:00 a.m. to 5:00 p.m.

Closed: Christmas Day and New Year's Day

Admission: $10 adult, $5 children 4–12 years old, seniors and military. Kama 'āina rates: $6 adults and $3 keiki, kupuna and military. Free admission for children 3 years and younger.

Guided Hikes: Guided activities are offered throughout the day: native plant walk, Hawaiian moorhen interpretation, historic walk, Hawaiian games, hula, etc. Check the schedule when you purchase your entrance ticket.

Facilities: Ample restrooms, drinking fountains, rain shelters, nature store, snack bar.

They're around, but more so in the evenings

50 inches

1,800 acres

Swimming in the waterfall pond

sea level to 1,000 feet

Wide paved main path, narrow dirt and gravel auxiliary paths, stone steps

Slippers

Waimea Valley has taken several names and played many roles throughout its significant history. In pre- and post-contact, the valley was home to a large population of native Hawaiians who took advantage of the valley's reliable fresh water for agriculture and excellent fishing grounds in the bay, until 1898 when a flood destroyed their crops and homes, displacing nearly 1,000 residents. During that time it was also a highly revered spiritual center surrounded by three major heiau. In more recent years it has served as a nature preserve and tourist attraction, popular for its cliff diving and hula exhibitions.

Today, the valley is one of O'ahu's last partially intact ahupua'a, native Hawaiian land use system. In addition to the 36 major botanical collections situated in the narrow valley that continue to thrive, educate and enthrall plant lovers, Waimea Valley is a bastion

The entrance to the gardens, restaurant and gift shop.

left: Lily pads spread across the tranquil fresh water and soak up the sun's energy to produce a magnificent flower. right: At one time, Waimea Valley was a flourishing ancient living site. Some areas have been restored for educational purposes.

for the preservation and continuation of Hawaiian spirituality and tradition, rich with cultural sites and traditional agricultural practices in use.

The plant collections include specific plant family plantings as well as regional plantings, but the main focus is on native Hawaiian plants, Polynesian introductions, and plants of island ecosystems. There are also several lily ponds and the Kamananui Stream—which contains four of five species of native freshwater fish—meandering from Waihī Falls all the way to Waimea Bay. The arboretum

The Kuʻula Shrine is an ancient fishing shrine.

contains more than 5,000 species of tropical plants in total.

You're greeted straight away as you pull into the parking lot by Hale O Lono, a heiau dedicated to Lono, the god of agriculture, weather, medicine and peace. From the parking lot, walk in between the snack bar and the nature store and be amazed as the grounds open up in front of you with the far-reaching canopy of monkeypod shading a lovely picnic lawn, bordered by flowering plants and palms. Just past the snack bar is a small native fern display. Keep an eye out for the beautiful plumage of several peacocks that call the valley home. One friendly male is known to flaunt his plumage for the camera.

Once you pass through the center entrance, on the left are several lily ponds surrounded by native Hawaiian flora. The plants are well labeled with placards that not only tell the name and origin, but also the use and significance of the plant in native Hawaiian culture. There are even a few koi fish swimming around the floating pads and ruffled white and pink flowers of several types of water lily. While you're by the lily ponds, check out the Kūʻula Stones, a model of an ancient fishing shrine.

The main road crosses the Kamananui Stream and gradually gains elevation as you make your way back toward the 40-foot waterfall. The distance from the park entrance to the waterfall is about a three-quarter-mile hike. There are plenty of bathroom stops and benches along the way, but it's a good idea to slather up with sunscreen and bring plenty of water. If you need to fill up your water bottle, there are two drinking fountains along the main road at the Ancient Hawaiian Living Site and the Hawaiian Games Site.

At the beginning of the main road is the collection of hibiscus, both true species and cultivars. The multi-colored blooms burst out from serrated leaves and many of the plants are the size of small trees, awash in color. Informative placards describe the origin of the cultivars. Past the hibiscus on the right is the Kauhale Ancient Hawaiian Living Site, a level area of rocks and ti, sheltered from the sun by a canopy of monkeypod and kukui trees.

left: Water lily. right: Flower of the cannonball tree.

left: Bromeliad garden. right: Sacred Hale Iwi, the burial site of a high priest or chief.

The main road continues on, flanked by canopy trees jutting up from the stream down below in the ravine and plants from the tropical Americas. There is also a trail that follows the stream almost the entire way to the waterfall from the lily ponds, just follow the Malesian Flora trail to find it. On the other side of the road are food plants, a planting of bromeliceae that grows on trees as well as in the ground, and sacred Hale Iwi, a 40- by 30-foot platform of stacked boulders that is believed to have been the burial place of a high priest or chief.

There are smaller auxiliary trails all over the place that branch off the main road and snake around other collections of plants and cultural sites. Do yourself

left: Ti cultivars. right: The hibiscus garden features both true species and cultivars.

The heavy, spherical fruit of the cannonball tree hangs from specialized branches on the trees trunk. Keep your distance.

a favor and take as many of the smaller paths as possible, they offer botanical glimpses into faraway tropical regions and are quieter and less traveled than the main path.

When you hit the fork in the main road, you're getting close to the falls. For a direct route, stay to your left. To explore a colorful and flower-filled section of the garden, take the right fork. There you'll find the heliconias and gingers: broad green leaves rising high off thick fibrous stalks with red, yellow and orange waxy flowers dangling and perched amongst the leaves. The variety of heliconia is amazing, all different types and colors of flower thriving under a cathedral canopy of tropical fruit trees like mango and cashew.

If the walk has left you exhausted, a last chance snack bar is your saving

top: The swimming hole at the falls is thirty feet deep. Exhibition cliff diving used to be an attraction in the past, but is now prohibited. bottom left: An auxiliary trail. bottom center: Ginger inflorescence. bottom right: Tropical foliage.

grace up by the waterfall. Cross the bridge and you're there. It takes about 18 hours to see the effect of a hard rain on the flow of the falls, which can be from a raging monster to a trickle. Swimming in the pond is limited depending on the amount of water making the drop. At its deepest point of 30 feet, the pond offers a great way to cool off and relax in a natural and prized setting.

Maui

- Mosquitoes
- Average Annual Rainfall
- Acres
- Best Known For
- Elevation
- Terrain
- Slippers or Shoes?

Enchanting Floral Gardens

2505 Kula Highway, Kula, Hawai'i 96790

Contact: (808) 878-2531, info@flowersofmaui.com, www.flowersofmaui.com

Directions: Located on the Kula Highway (37) at mile marker 10.

Hours Daily: 9:00 a.m. to 5:00 p.m.

Admission: $7.50 per person, $5 seniors 65 and over, $1 children 5 to 11 years old.

Guided Hikes: Self-guided tours only.

Facilities: Restrooms, book and gift shop.

Weddings: Three gazebos available to choose from.

Bring the bug spray, for sure

8 inches

8 acres

Proteas and exotic flowers

2,500 feet

Flat paved path

Slippers

Just below the town of Kula on the west-facing slope of Haleakalā, the Enchanting Floral Gardens shows over 2000 species of tropical and semi-tropical plants from around the world. Mr. Takeda, owner, horticulturist and award-winning petunia breeder, purchased the once small garden in 1992 with only 300 tropical plants and developed his garden through cuttings and seed over the years. Today the garden is rich in fruit trees, flower and fragrance, with a great deal of the collection hailing from Africa and Australia as well some native Hawaiian plant species.

Because the garden is practically level, it's hard to tell how far back onto the property you've strolled; a different fruit tree or flowering plant is around every bend. The thick foliage lining both sides of the paved pathway keeps your focus on what's immediately in front of you and the painted yellow arrows on the ground keep you moving in the right direction along the twisting, snaking path.

left: A colorful collection of coleus greets visitors to the garden. right: The Mayday protea is a robust hybrid cultivated in upcountry Maui and admired for its large flower.

Sago palm and bananas rise above the ground cover.

Halfway through the garden the silver, felt-like leaves of the licorice plant add texture to the garden.

left: Different varieties of taro in the garden, including the charcoal black leaves of the Black Magic variety, are able to grow well in soil. right: Just a few of the 2,400 different species of Bromeriaceae.

Because of the cooler temperatures found at 2,500 feet on the Haleakalā volcano, many different plants than usually seen throughout Hawai'i's botanical garden's thrive in this climate. Gangly begonias, bright-colored coleus and tropical rhododendrons, with dainty orange flowers, all thrive in the drier leeward climate. The bulbous and prickly looking flower of the hearty protea is peppered throughout this garden and many different varietals are represented.

The garden boasts over 50 fruit trees including white sapote, pomelo, avocado, guava, pumpkin cherry, pomegranate, lychee and mango to name a few. And while the flowers and trees may be spread evenly throughout the garden, there are also themed plantings to accent the blooming foliage. A small 'awa patch grows under a towering koa tree, flanked by yellow 'ōhi'a lehua, kukui and coastal sandalwood. Ponds provide a watery home for day and night blooming lilies. Bromeliads and orchids grow side by side on hapu'u fern logs. A succulent garden contains many varieties of agave, the curious pencil cactus tree, and the unique aloe tree, reaching 15 feet into the air. The clumps of Chinese and Mexican bamboo are a visitor favorite and a wide variety of palm trees accompany the landscape.

The trail through the garden is easy to follow and offers a beautiful view of Ma'alaea Bay and Kaho'olawe from the center of the garden. There are a few plant identification signs, which display the common and scientific plant names in both English and Japanese. If you're lucky, you might catch Mr. Takeda out in the garden and if there's one thing he loves to do, it's talk about plants.

left: A place to picnic under a guava tree. right: A pincushion flower, a member of the protea family. These native South African plants thrive in upcountry Maui.

Hāna Maui Botanical Garden

470 Ulaino Road, P.O. Box 404, Hāna, Hawai'i 96713

Contact: (808) 248-7725, JoLoyce@aol.com

Directions: Coming from Kahului, turn left off the Hāna Highway (36) and onto Ulaino Road. Drive down the road one mile and the garden is on the right.

Hours Daily: 9:00 a.m. to 5:00 p.m.

Admission: $3 per person

Guided Hikes: Self-guided tours, maps are provided.

Facilities: Vacation studio rentals.

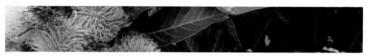

Oh yeah, watch out!

~120 inches

27 acres, 10 of which make up the garden

Fruit trees

Sea level

Natural grass over smooth, flat lava

Slippers are fine unless you don't like getting your feet wet

Established in 1976 as a vacation rental tourist destination, the 10-acre garden was carved out of the 27-acre seaside property and opened to the public in 1986. Hāna Maui Botanical Garden is a hodgepodge of canoe plants, ornamental tropical flowering plants, fruit trees and even a few Hawaiian native species.

The garden is spread out across the property in a curious fashion, one that lends itself to exploration. It is planted in large clumps of plants—several fruit trees surrounded by gingers, heliconia, ti or other exotic flowering plants, with small trails in between foliage and flower. From one open space, duck through a tunnel of heliconia leaves to pop out into another grassy clearing, with large fruit trees and more flowers around. The garden is like a giant maze, with several trails to choose from in any open space you come into, except there's no need to fear getting lost. If the handwritten map seems a little jumbled and confusing, just walk back toward the mountains and you'll end up where you started.

left: Hāna Maui Botanical Garden is full of fruit for the picking: lychee. right: Too many star fruit to count.

Fruit trees sprout up everywhere—guava, sapote, avocado, tangelo, Samoan mountain apple, mango, and macadamia nut are just a few. If you can't find it, it's probably not planted here. When the fruit is ripe for the picking and close enough to the ground to reach, go for it. There are all kinds of exotic fruits growing throughout the garden. Many varieties of palm trees also grace the garden with a majority of coconut palms, so look out above.

Ginger, heliconia and other tropical ornamentals cloak the base of the fruit trees and palms.

The best way to tackle this garden is to simply pick a path and wander around, loosely following the garden layout on the map. There are very few signs identifying the plants and 12 red-painted, numbered coconuts that correspond to different sections of the garden. Another way to orient yourself is to traverse to the middle of the garden, where a thick wall of areca palms thrive, and head out in all directions from there, using the palms as a central point to track your progress.

top left and right: Concealed trails open up to small clearings with fruit and flower all around. bottom: A breadfruit tree towers above red ti and bananas.

Low key and off the beaten path, the garden resides in a natural state of overgrown abundance and the grass underfoot seems to be the only thing manicured. Most of the garden grows thick, the small open spaces giving only temporary room to expand your view to the sky. The west side of the garden, however, is the opposite. Tall and mature kukui trees, monkeypod, avocado and breadfruit give shelter across a wide spreading open lawn space, great for a picnic or just taking in a deep breathe of fresh Hāna air and relaxing under a beautiful canopy.

If the kids need a break from the car, this is the place to let them spread their wings, run around and explore.

top: Small white flowers emerge from the red bracts of this ginger inflorescence. bottom: Looking back towards the mountains, rhapis palm front and center.

Kahanu Garden (National Tropical Botanical Garden)

'Ula'ino Rd., Hāna, Hawai'i, 96713

Contact: NTBG Administrative offices (on Kaua'i) (808) 332-7324, www.ntbg.org/gardens/kahanu.php, administration@ntbg.org, Kahanu Garden info line (808) 248-8912

Directions: Located on the Hāna Highway near Hāna at mile marker 31. Turn left onto 'Ula'ino Road, continue for 1.1 miles, crossing a streambed. The entrance is marked by a sign on the gate.

Hours Daily: Monday – Friday, 10:00 a.m. to 2:00 p.m. Saturday by reservation only.

Closed: Sundays

Admission: $10 per person, children 12 and under are free.

Guided Hikes: Half-mile self-guided tour, takes from one to two hours. Two-hour guided hike Saturday mornings at 10 a.m., $25, children 12 and under are free.

Facilities: Restrooms, no drinking water.

Very abundant

120 inches

Nearly 300 acres of which roughly 40 acres are open to the public

The Pi'ilanihale Heiau

Sea level

Level grass

Slippers are fine, but the grass is often wet

Step back in time on this sacred site that is steeped in rich Hawaiian history. Kahanu Garden has been home to Hawaiian kings and chiefs, and today continues its role as a perpetuator of culture with an ethnobotanical garden of Polynesian canoe plants, east Maui plants, a hala preserve, and the largest remaining heiau, Pi'ilanihale, in the Hawaiian Islands.

Once you check in at the visitor kiosk, the garden opens up before you with 'ulu (breadfruit) trees all around. The grove is home to more than 120 different varieties of the tall and wide stretching tree, the most diverse collection in the world. With broad and leathery leaves that can grow to three feet long and fruit that can weigh up to ten pounds, take time to find the nuances between the many different varieties growing in the garden. And make sure to take heed of falling breadfruit.

top and bottom: From just about anywhere in the garden, the Piʻilanihale Heiau dominates the landscape. Built in stages beginning as early as the 13th century, the heiau is a strong reminder of an advanced ancient civilization.

There is a maintenance building on the left and the bathroom is located on the left-hand side. Plantings of maile, 'awa, hapu'u fern and other native plants adorn the base of breadfruit and kukui trees around the structure. Drive past the maintenance building, staying on the cement driveway to a parking area about a quarter mile across a large field. Tall and mature exotic trees line the opposite side of the field, the "modern introduction" area of Kahanu Garden.

Kahanu Garden was originally part of a thriving ancient living site and with its abundant rainfall and fertile soil, developed into an important agricultural area. The ahupua'a (land division) of Honomā'ele thrived over the centuries and under the peaceful and prosperous rule of Ali'i Pi'ilani, who united all of Maui during the 16th century, Hāna became one of the royal centers of the kingdom as well as spiritual centers with the construction of the heiau at Honomā'ele, the name of the bay, as well.

In 1848, when the Hawaiian Monarchy established private land ownership, half of the ahupua'a of Honomā'ele, about 990 acres, was given to Chief Kahanu by King Kamehameha III. Portions of the ahupua'a endured several land-use

The rugged and verdant black rock coastline of the north shore of Maui.

Utility stones and ti.

changes, but stayed in the Kahanu ʻohana—from the 1860s till 1946 the land was a thriving sugar plantation, then switched gears to pasture for grazing cattle until 1974, when the Kahanu family and Hāna Ranch deeded 61 acres to establish the Kahanu Garden.

At the parking area, walk under the hau bush and emerge in the canoe garden of a Hawaiʻi of yesteryear, with ʻawa, banana, bottle gourd, sweet potato, taro, sugarcane and many other plants used in traditional Hawaiian culture. The purpose of the garden is not only a place to research and cultivate these plants, but to educate, preserve and share, a repository of purposeful plants for the community.

The breadfruit grove is home to more than 120 different varieties of breadfruit tree. With different size and shapes of leaf and fruit, the breadfruit was important part of the ancient Hawaiian diet.

Follow the row of sugarcane and kamani trees that leads to your first stunning and awe inspiring view of the heiau. Massive, strong and evoking a spiritual presence below the verdant mountains, Pi'ilanihale Heiau is believed to have been built in stages as early as the 13th century. The dry-laid stone structure was cleared off and restored over the last four decades and is under perpetual care of the garden. The heiau dominates the rest of the garden, always standing proud and in clear view from all other points in the main garden area fringing the ocean.

Stay to the left, and walk towards Honomā'ele Bay, with a small cliff and the ocean to your left. You'll come upon Hale Ho'okipa, a rain shelter with some information inside on the walls. Different types of utility stones, a grinding stone, mortars and an anchor stone surround the dwelling. Look through the hala and shrubs on the side of the cliff and sneak some great views looking northwest along the rugged and rocky coast.

Continue up toward Kalāhū Point to the rickety and weathered cottage, a fishing hut built in the 1940s, and have a look inside at the different artifacts and old pictures. From here, skirt back across the lawn hugging the coconut collection on the shoreline without getting too close as to suffer a substantial knock on the noggin from a falling coconut. Planted among the hala and palms are east Maui native plant species. With the energy and aura of the heiau on your right, the parking area is all the way across the lawn and past the canoe plants. As you look across the sprawling grass field, try to image the sugarcane plantation, the cattle pasture and the thriving and fertile gardens of the ancient Hawaiians.

Native plants endemic to Maui fill the nooks and crannies of this ancient lava flow that runs parallel to the rocky beach right behind the hala tree.

Ke'anae Arboretum

Near mile marker 16, Ke'anae, Maui

Directions: The arboretum is on the mauka side (mountain side) of the road, in between mile marker 16 and 17 on the Hāna Highway (36). Limited parking available on both sides of the road by the arboretum sign. Do not block the gate.

Hours Daily: Dawn until dusk

Admission: Free

Guided Hikes: Self-guided, one-and-a-half mile (one-way) hike.

Facilities: None

Yes

~100 inches

6 acres

Tall trees

~120 feet

Smooth paved trail with a small section of narrow rocky and uneven, grass path

Slippers

Driving the Hāna Highway is an arduous task. It takes heightened awareness and maintained focus to navigate the unrelenting tight turns, all the while watching out for oncoming traffic on the notoriously narrow two-lane (and often one-lane) road. Located in between mile marker 16 and 17, nearly half way to Hāna town, the Ke'anae Arboretum is a great stop to stretch your legs, revitalize the senses and check out some beautiful, tall and mature trees.

Ke'anae Arboretum not only features exotic trees and native Hawaiian plants, but the air is laced with the eye-opening fragrance of thousands of ginger blooms erupting trailside, a perfumey aroma with a hint of spice. The yellow ginger gives way to lemon eucalyptus and fragrant puakenikeni trees farther down the trail, the floral scent of flowers wafting by with the breeze. The entirety of the walk is punctuated by lovely and arresting botanical scents.

From the roadside, the wide, paved walkway runs parallel to a stream down below, and is pinned in a valley with the rocky wall of the rising mountain on

left: Ke'anae Arboretum is home to many types of mature exotic trees and palms. right: Looking skyward up the colorful, wavy trunks of the Mindanao gum stand.

the other. African tulip trees, monkeypod and kukui trees spread overhead and shade the path as ginger thrives in the streambed, concealing the water from sight and replacing it with a barrage to another of the five senses. Breadfruit and eucalyptus trees also make a presence.

Pass through another gate and into the arboretum proper. Palms from around the tropics are dispersed between tall trees through out the arboretum and most of the plants are signed for identification. The natural ground cover and sporadic palm plantings try to distract the viewer from noticing that many of the trees of the same species, planted in small stands, are actually planted in linear rows. The stand of 12 teak trees (known for their hard wood) with broad, round green leaves is a rare sight for most people.

The path meanders under the canopy of exotic trees, a noteworthy stand of rainbow eucalyptus or painted gum trees, from the rainforests of Mindanao in the Philippines, attracts a curious gaze. As the bark peels from the entire length of the trunk in random strips, it reveals a new color of bark, from red and orange to green and purple. The sleek trunks bend and snake 150 feet toward the sky.

left: Lemon-scented eucalyptus really do give off a light, yet very noticeable lemon scent.
right: The peeling bark of the Mindanao gum gives way to many colors of the rainbow.

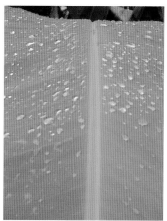

Beaded dewdrops on a large green leaf are reminiscent of a recent rain, commonplace along the road to Hāna.

Pass by the cane palm and out from the underneath the shady canopy. The sun is unobstructed, if it isn't raining, and green ti lines the now uneven and rocky path, hidden beneath clumps of grass. The path becomes very rocky so take your time and remember to look down every once in a while to gauge the condition of the trail. The valley walls are covered in kukui and breadfruit trees. At the end of the ti planting is a taro patch with many Hawaiian varieties. Pass through the gate in the fence and continue for another mile into the natural rainforest of the area.

Kula Botanical Garden

638 Kekaulike Avenue, Kula, Hawai'i 96790

Contact: (808) 878-1715 www.kulabotanicalgarden.com

Directions: Located on the Kekaulike Highway (377) near the Kula Highway (37) junction. Turn left from Highway 37 after Rice Park onto Highway 377. There is a sign and a steep driveway less than a mile ahead on your right.

Hours Daily: 9:00 a.m. to 4:00 p.m.

Admission: $7.50 adult, $2.00 children 6 to 12, children under 6 are free

Guided Hikes: Tours are self-guided, but guided hikes can be arranged with advance notice. There is a $45 tour guide fee plus admission, but also a price break on admission for parties of 13 or more at $8.00 per person. There is also an agriculture tour of the 9-acre Christmas tree and coffee farm by appointment only.

Facilities: Gift shop, snack bar, restrooms and open-air deck with a view.

Weddings: Several locations that can accommodate from 4 to 150 people. Chairs, tables and tents are available for rent.

There are many curious facets to this upcountry botanical garden that make it unique, interesting and infused with character, starting with its inception. In 1969, landscape architect Warren McCord and his wife purchased the original 10-acre plot, which was covered with the invasive black wattle tree, mainly because of the unique rock formations on the property. With vision and a lot of elbow grease, the two botanical enthusiasts cleared the land and made the initial plantings of the Kula Botanical Garden, which opened to the public in 1971. Their goal was to provide a natural garden of exotic and native plants that grow at high elevation in Hawai'i.

It was McCord's mission from the start to preserve the natural rock formations, of which 17 layers of geologic activity are apparent, and incorporate them into a showcase garden. Today, the sinew of rock that runs the length of the garden has been transformed into a rushing stream with waterfalls, koi ponds and caves. The garden is bursting with all types of botanicals, from ground covers and flowers to

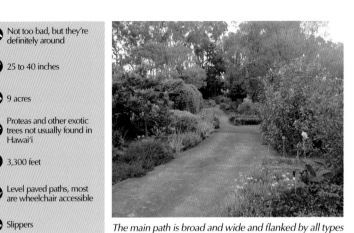

Not too bad, but they're definitely around

25 to 40 inches

9 acres

Proteas and other exotic trees not usually found in Hawai'i

3,300 feet

Level paved paths, most are wheelchair accessible

Slippers

The main path is broad and wide and flanked by all types of interesting plants and flowers.

small shrubs and mature trees. In fact, all the mature trees thriving in the garden are a product of his initial planting some 35 years ago.

From the quaint gift shop, there is a main walkway that extends all the way to the back of the garden and smaller loop paths continually originate from either side. Heading up the slight incline of the garden, the bromeliad garden under a shade house is on the path to your right, flower spikes of red and purple punctuate the setting. On the other side of the main trail is a spreading lawn bordered by colorful ginger and hibiscus.

Many varieties of protea thrive in this upcountry botanical garden.

Continuing up the property, colorful blooms of protea sprout up all around. There's even a planting of blue hydrangea with big, cotton candy balls of flowers. Of particular interest in the center of the garden is the twisted and gnarled banksia tree, a native of Australia. The mature specimen has seven trunks sprouting from its base, all twisting in their own wonky directions. The flowers resemble large bottle brushes, but even more curious is the trunk. It appears to be nubby and bumpy and the color of rust. The bumps are a characteristic of this type of banksia, but the rust color

left: A stream flows gently through the garden and terminates at the ginger-cloaked koi pond. right: Brightly colored ornamentals and tall-reaching flowers border the main lawn area often used for weddings.

Hydrangea blossom in the foreground as a twisted and gnarled banksia tree, native to Australia, sends out seven lanky trunks from its base.

left: The gazebo at the back of the garden overlooks several ponds where nene geese, cranes and Cayuga ducks enjoy their very own bird sanctuary. right: A one-of-a-kind deciduous tree for Hawai'i, the prehistoric Ginkgo biloba. The cool climate in upcountry Maui is just right for this unique tree.

comes from the colony of lichen that has attached to the trunk and thrives in all the moist nooks and pockets.

Past the banksia tree is a small gazebo under a kukui tree, a quiet place to gaze over the wash that runs the length of the property, which is normally dry unless the rains are heavy. Continue up the slight grade to find the orchid house and the bird sanctuary, home to two Hawaiian nene geese, two grey-crowned cranes and three Cayuga ducks. Jacarandas stretch their canopy over the bird sanctuary and send out purple clumps of flowers.

Heading back down the garden on the right side of the trail, fuchsias are a special find, their hanging basket flowers swaying in the breeze. There is a "tabu garden" of poisonous plants and next to the covered bridge is a rare find in Hawai'i, the deciduous ginkgo biloba tree, the evolutionary link between ferns and conifers, a living fossil. Only at this elevation will the tree survive in the tropics.

Next up are the koi ponds with two covered areas for sitting and relaxing. Surrounded by ginger, its scent is thick in the air, powerful and invigorating.

The garden has several varieties of eucalyptus and pine trees, including the Monterey Pine, which the McCords farm for Christmas trees on an adjoining 9-acre parcel. Native Hawaiian plants are also sprinkled throughout the garden.

Maui Nui Botanical Gardens

P.O. Box 6040, 150 Kanaloa Ave., Kahului, Hawai'i 96732

Contact: (808) 249-2798, info@mnbg.org, www.mnbg.org

Directions: Turn onto Kanaloa Avenue in Kahului from either W. Kaahumanu Avenue or Kahului Beach Road The garden is across from the War Memorial Football and Baseball Stadiums.

Hours Daily: Monday – Saturday from 8:00 a.m. to 4:00 p.m.

Closed: Sundays and major holidays

Admission: Free

Guided Hikes: Self-guided tour. Stop by the office for a site map and to make a donation.

Facilities: Restrooms, picnic tables, playground.

Not at this garden

12 to 20 inches

5 acres

Emphasizing the plants of Maui Nui (Maui, Moloka'i, Lāna'i and Kaho'olawe)

Sea level

Flat

Slippers

Located less than a mile from the shoreline of Kahului Bay, Maui Nui Botanical Gardens is a prime example of a coastal climate garden growing Hawaiian native species and Polynesian introductions exclusively (except for the massive banyan tree in the center of the lawn, which in accordance with the lease, cannot be removed). Over thirty years in existence, this garden was the first in the state of Hawai'i to focus their attention solely on native species and their cultural significance.

The ethnobotanical garden is generously spread across the five-acre property that many years ago was a zoo. Winding paved paths, a large central lawn area, restroom facilities and several small, three-sided dwellings are all that remain. In place of exotic animals are now plants found in the severely declining dryland ecosystems of Maui, Moloka'i, Lāna'i, and Kaho'olawe, and plants used by native Hawaiian peoples for food and medicinal, building and clothing purpose.

top: Hala stands watch over smaller plantings of Hawai'i natives, including the native white hibiscus. bottom: This planting near the entrance of the garden is signed for plant identification and Hawaiian name.

left: Shaded picnic areas are located throughout the garden. right: Kō, sugarcane, was used for food and medicine.

With over 40 varieties of sugarcane (kō) with colorful stalks ranging from yellow to red and purple, 70 varieties of taro (kalo) and 25 rare banana (mai'a) varieties thriving, this garden is at the forefront of cultural perpetuation in Hawai'i. The garden works with state and private agencies growing endangered native species for restoration efforts and is associated with the County of Maui Board of Water Supply to promote xeriscape gardening—landscaping with

left: Mai'a minini is the only variegated banana in the world. The leaves, trunk and fruit all exhibit interesting striped patterns. right: A field of ipu, gourds. Its cultural uses included water and food containers as well as a musical instrument to accompany hula.

left: 'Ohe makai flowers blossom from a plant native to dry forests in Hawai'i. right: The fragrant flower of the koki'o ke'oke'o, a hibiscus native to Moloka'i.

water thrifty plants suited for a particular climate. In addition, the garden also conducts native plant sales and native tree giveaways on Arbor Day.

Because in a coastal dune zone, salt spray, steady tradewinds and little rain are conditions the garden must contend with. But with xeriscape gardening techniques in place, the garden is thriving. Most of the native plants are planted in raised clumps with mulch, ground covers, small shrubs and flowering plants growing side by side. Loulu palms are planted throughout and there is even endemic sandalwood, 'iliahi. Larger trees like kukui and milo give shade to the bordering regions of the garden and offer quiet spots to relax and enjoy a respite from the sun.

The layout of the garden is straightforward and because of the large, central grass area and the clustered plantings, you can see all around the rectangular property from most points in the garden. The bulk of the flowering plant collection, like mai'a pilo with its fragrant white blossoms, koki'o ke'oke'o (white hibiscus from Moloka'i), 'ilima and pua kala, one of the few native plants with thorns, are directly beyond the main office at the entrance. A few other group plantings that include Hawai'i's state flower, ma'o hau hele, a beautiful hibiscus that is nearly extinct in the wild, are located on the other side of the bathrooms on the street side of the garden.

Completely across the garden, on the opposite side of the central lawn, are taro, gourd and sugarcane plantings. Banana trees sprout up among the other canoe plants and hala dots the entire property. Make sure you check out the manini banana, with variegated leaves and bananas. It's one of a kind in Hawai'i and it tastes pretty good, too.

Hawai'i

- Mosquitoes
- Average Annual Rainfall
- Acres
- Best Known For
- Elevation
- Terrain
- Slippers or Shoes?

Amy B. H. Greenwell Ethnobotanical Garden

P.O. Box 1053, 82-6188 Mamalohoa Highway, Captain Cook, Hawai'i 96704

Contact: (808) 323-3318 agg@bishopmuseum.org,
www.bishopmuseum.org/exhibits/greenwell/greenwell.html

Directions: Located 12 miles south of Kailua-Kona on Highway 11 in Captain Cook. The entrance to the garden is on the mauka side of the road near mile marker 110.

Hours Daily: Monday – Saturday from 8:30 a.m. to 5:00 p.m.

Closed: Sunday and holidays

Admission: Suggested donation for adults is $5. Self-guided tours are free. Guided tours are $5.

Guided Hikes: Half-hour to hour self-guided tours and additional guided tours are available on Wednesday and Friday at 1:00 p.m. and a special guided tour is offered at no charge on the second Saturday of every month at 10:00 a.m.

Facilities: Restrooms and cold drinking water.

Not too bad

~50 inches

15 acres

Kona Field System

~1,400 feet

Level gravel and grass pathways, also uneven and steep grass and gravel paths and steps

Shoes

The Amy Greenwell Ethnobotanical Garden is a well-preserved cultural heritage site and home to many native and endangered plants of west Hawai'i Island. Through a natural dispersal of the trees and plants, the garden changes dramatically as it rises in elevation, reflective of the different climate zones that exist in Hawai'i and the native plants that grow (or once grew) there.

At the heart of the garden is the preservation of long stone ridges, remnants of the Kona Field System. Utilized by ancient Hawaiian farmers, the stone ridges, kuaiwi, that ran up and down the slopes of the mountain marked boundaries of fields and created a vast agriculture complex in upland Kona, spreading over 18 miles long and three miles wide. The skilled farmers planted their main crops, like taro and sweet potato, inbetween the ridges

top: In the agricultural zone of the garden, nanea (in the foreground) is used as a green manure. bottom left: Ancient Hawaiian farmers laid out the fields up and down the slopes and lined them with stone and plants like ti and sugarcane. bottom right: A very rare hibiscus relative, Kokia cookei, *relies on special care from botanical experts to survive.*

and planted ti and sugarcane along the edges, using the old leaves as mulch. Breadfruit trees were also a common crop. The kuaiwi found at Amy Greenwell Garden are about 500 years old.

The stone ridges, or kuaiwi, provided a stone-mulched planting surface in addition to the fields. In this field, ki grows in the kuaiwi beside a field of wauke.

Several wide mounds of Kona stone, flanked by ti and sugarcane, run up the slope to the koa upland forest. Tall and slender 'ōhi'a lehua trees with small round leaves and bushy red blossoms gracefully stand watch over the agricultural site. In ancient times the koa forest was much more expansive, but the mature koa trees that form the modern day canopy across the slope's ridgeline offers a window to the dynamic and useful forest that once carpeted the upland regions. To access the trail that snakes through the koa forest, just walk up the grass in between the stone ridges and you can pick up the trail at either end of the koa stand. Along the shady forest walk you'll find hapu'u fern, native white hibiscus and benches to sit among many other native plants.

Below the kuaiwi is the lowland dry forest plant section. Rare and endangered Hawaiian trees and shrubs are spaced across a grassy field. Very rare koki'o, with large, red peeled back flowers, *Kokia cookei*, which no longer grow from seed and rare west Hawai'i loulu palms are featured in this section. Uhi uhi, halapepe, 'a'ali'i, small wiliwili trees and native Hawaiian gardenia accentuate the grouped plantings.

Down by the road, at the lowest elevation of the property, is the coastal zone planting. Dominated by tall trees, like kukui and kamani, as well as coconut palms, most of the plants here are found throughout the shores of Polynesia. But natives like hau and naupaka are also present.

While the garden is visible from the highway, actually finding the small parking area can be tricky. If you're coming from the north, look for mile marker 110. Once you see the small sign on the mauka side of the road, turn into the driveway that is right before the garden's modest sign. Go up the gravel road until you see the small white visitor center and plant nursery. There is a small gravel parking area to the right. If you're coming from the south, turn right onto the narrow road just after the garden's sign.

left: This rare native fan palm, Pritchardia schattaueri, *is one of nearly 300 federally listed endangered species in Hawai'i. right: Mai'a, Hawaiian bananas (*Musa sp.*), are normally cooked.*

Hawai'i Tropical Botanical Garden

P.O. Box 80, 27-717 Old Mamalahoa Highway, Papa'ikou, Hawai'i 96781

Contact: (808) 964-5233 htbg@ilhawaii.net www.hawaiigarden.com

Directions: From the Mamalahoa Highway (Hwy 19) take the 4 Mile Scenic Route (Old Mamalahoa Highway). The garden is located at Onomea Bay.

Hours Daily: 9:00 a.m. to 5:00 p.m., last admission ending at 4:00 p.m.

Closed: Thanksgiving Day, Christmas Day and New Year's Day

Admission: $15 adult, $5 children (ages 16 – 6), children 5 and under are free. Yearly and lifetime passes available.

Guided Hikes: One mile, one-and-a-half-hour self-guided tour available. Golf cart assistance is available on the boardwalk to the lookout.

Facilities: Visitor center, gift shop, restrooms, refreshments and snacks.

Weddings: Packages available, contact (808) 964-5233.

They're around

~130 inches

40 acres

Onomea Falls and large collection of rare, wild collected heliconia and ginger

150 feet to sea level

Level, paved pathways, inclined walkways and stairs

Slippers

The Onomea Valley has had a long and colorful history, from the legend of King Kamehameha throwing his spear to form the Onomea Arch (that crumbled during a 1956 earthquake) on the north side of Onomea Bay to sugar mills, farms and cattle grazing. The picturesque valley and bay held court as a Hawaiian fishing village, called Kahali'i, and also as the Big Island's first natural landing area for sailing ships. Unfortunately, early settlers left quite a destructive footprint and removed all of the valley's vegetation.

The valley saw a period of rapid regrowth in the early 1900s, but it wasn't until Dan Lutkenhouse purchased the land in 1977 and devoted the next eight years of his life to creating the gardens

The elevated, wooden path snakes down the ravine, in and above the tropical foliage.

that exist for your enjoyment today. Trails were forged and the location of every plant was meticulously scrutinized. By the time the garden opened to the public in 1984, over 2,000 species of tropical plants from all over the world were thriving in this rain-soaked valley. Today, the botanical garden doubles as a living seed bank for tropical and subtropical gardens around the world.

After checking in at the visitor center, carefully cross the two-lane road and descend down a twisting flight of wooden stairs running between Kahaliʻi Stream and Onomea Stream. The rainforest ravine pulses with the sound of rushing water and birdsong, the smell of rain-soaked foliage and earth thick in the nostrils. The ravine is full of white star ginger and heliconia, while pink quill tillandsia poke colorful flower spikes out from the mossy ravine wall. Towering palms line the far side of the ravine.

Palms are a big draw in this garden. There are more than 200 species of palm, some of which are over 100 years old, like the Australian Alexandra palms that dominate the topography surrounding Onomea Falls.

At the bottom of the stairs the trail splits. Take the left fork, the Palm Jungle Trail, past the jackfruit tree to the lookout at the foot of Onomea Falls. This gradual three-tiered falls leisurely spills down three rocky drop-offs, ferns and mottled mosses cover everything in sight, palms abound. The scenery has a soft, velvety allure.

Follow Onomea Stream onto the Heliconia Trail, where broad leaves reach well overhead and waxy blooms hang down to entice pollinators. As you walk, heliconia in the foreground, guava trees in the background, you begin to notice waves rolling into the bay through the foliage, a sneak peek of more to come.

Up next is the orchid garden and bird aviary with six South American Macaws. You'll also find Bromeliad Hill, aptly named because of the profusion of bromeliads covering a small hill. Make sure to follow the sign out to Anthurium

Onomea Stream spills into the Pacific Ocean across a black sand beach.

Corner, which gets you right out to a stone's throw from the water; whitewater rolls up onto the rocky beach below.

Heliconia, calathea and croton borders Lily Lake, a small pond stocked with koi fish and water lilies. Cross a dirt road and roam under the canopy of mature monkeypod trees. This is Monkeypod Trail, where shade-loving foliage will take you out to the edge of the lava, to an unobstructed view of Onomea Bay and the surrounding headlands. Ironwood trees, spider lily and red spider lily line the coast as the water turbulently meets with the jagged lava below. Don't miss the blowhole as you walk south to the Ocean Vista.

At the far end of the Ocean Vista Trail, bordering the rocky beach where Alakahi Stream meets the Pacific Ocean, you'll take in Turtle Point and Crab Cove, where ironwood covered cliffs in the distance create a backdrop for the waves that crash on a jagged finger of lava protruding out in the ocean.

The Alakahi Stream Trail takes you under tropical almond trees and away from the ocean, the sound of the waves crashing onto the shore still soothes from a distance. To get a close look at the stream cross the small bridge and walk along the short Boulder Creek Trail. You also have the option of taking the Cook Pine trail, which terminates at a mature Cook pine, piercing the foliage and shooting toward the sky, one of the tallest trees in the valley.

top left: Very large, waxy heliconia inflorescence. top right: Onomea Falls. bottom left: Hanging lobster claw heliconia. bottom right: A sneak peak of the bay from the Heliconia Trail.

As you make your way back to the visitor center up the main trail, make sure to take in all the side loop trails, like the Torch Ginger Trail and Fern Circle. The garden caters to the cruise ships, bringing in guests all day long by the van load. So get there early if you want to experience the garden in its most peaceful and tranquil state. Not to mention it will be easier to get great pictures.

Manuka State Wayside

Office Contact: *75 Aupuni Street #204, Hilo, Hawai'i 96721*

Contact: (808) 974-6200

Directions: Located on the Mamalahoa Highway (Hwy 11) 41 miles south of Kona, just north of mile marker 81.

Hours Daily: 24 hours a day

Admission: Free

Guided Hikes: Not available, but the park is an access point to trails in the preserve.

Facilities: Restrooms and picnic tables, but no drinking water.

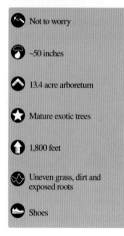

Not to worry

~50 inches

13.4 acre arboretum

Mature exotic trees

1,800 feet

Uneven grass, dirt and exposed roots

Shoes

When driving the southern section of the Hawai'i Belt Road between Kailua-Kona and Hilo, the Manuka State Wayside is a wonderful natural area to take a break from the drive, get out of the car, and stretch by taking a walk through the thriving and very unique arboretum. Colonel L. W. "Bill" Bryan and forestry workers created the wayside nearly 80 years ago. Initial plantings of forty-eight species of native Hawaiian plants and over 130 species of exotic plants were introduced into the upland 'ōhi'a lehua forest and continued for nearly two decades.

Today, the Manuka State Wayside is surrounded by the Manuka Natural Area Reserve, which covers 25,000 acres of the southwest flank of Mauna Loa volcano. The wayside park is also the trailhead of a two-mile loop trail that explores a swath of native Hawaiian forest with lava flows of different ages, a pit crater and cultural sites.

The natural old growth 'ōhi'a lehua forest dominates the landscape around the wayside park, which is split in two by the restroom and picnic facilities.

left: A trailhead is located at Manuka State Wayside. right: Exotic species with bulbous trunks.

left: Many different kinds of exotic trees spread their canopy over the wayside. right: The peeling bark of a eucalyptus tree litters the natural area.

left: Roots criss-cross the uneven ground under sickle-shaped leaves. right: Planted nearly 80 years ago, the mature trees, like the podocarpus on the right are able to reach their full potential.

On the west side of the parking lot, past the Hong Kong orchid trees, is an open, grassy area, dotted with hibiscus and small trees. On the east side of the parking lot is the arboretum.

The mature, exotic trees have grown tall with wide spreading canopies since their initial planting and the forest floor is crisscrossed with shallow roots spreading out in all directions. Existing in a natural state with leaf litter, dirt and sparse grass between the exposed roots systems, it's necessary to watch your step. People have the tendency to walk around looking up, potentially tripping over the knobby and twisted roots underfoot.

The many different species of trees, different types of trunks, bark, branches and foliage are a delight. Planted in close proximity to one another, it's interesting to see the striking differences between the small, blade-like leaves of the giant, weeping podocarpus trees, the spiky, segmented needles of Araucaria, the smooth bulbous trunk of the kapok, and the hundreds of aerial roots of the ficus. Unfortunately, there is no signage for identification.

The tranquility is noteworthy in the arboretum, punctuated by the calls of native birds like the 'elepaio, and the swoosh of intermittent motorists flying by on the highway below. The arboretum is a great place to escape the road for a brief time and explore the candy store of unique mature trees.

Nani Mau Gardens

421 Makalika Street, Hilo, Hawaiʻi 96720

Contact: (808) 959-3500 corp@hottours.us www.nanimaugardens.com

Directions: From Highway 11, turn onto Makalika Street, which is between mile markers 3 and 4.

Hours Daily: 10:00 a.m. to 3:00 p.m.

Admission: Garden admission: $10 adults, $5 children (4-10 years old). Garden and tram admission: $17 adults, $10 children (4-10 years old). Kama ʻaina rates are offered and garden admission with lunch rates are available. Special rates for groups over 10.

Guided Hikes: Self-guided garden tour and a half-hour narrated tram tour are offered.

Facilities: Restrooms, Restaurant, gift shop and art gallery.

Weddings: Indoor and outdoor facilities for weddings, banquets and special events. Call to (808) 959-3500 for arrangements.

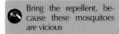 Bring the repellent, because these mosquitoes are vicious

 ~130 inches

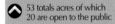 53 totals acres of which 20 are open to the public

 Orchid garden

 280 feet

 Level paved paths

 Slippers

The orchid pavilion displays hundreds of blooming orchids and other plants on rock platforms.

top: The banks of the stream that flows across one portion of the garden are planted with brightly colored flowering plants. bottom: A picturesque place to sit and relax in the main garden.

Some people prefer naturally styled gardens, where plants blend together as they would in nature. Others prefer a manicured, thoughtfully-designed garden, where each plant is strategically placed and every rock, statue or waterway is incorporated into the overall theme. Nani Mau Gardens resembles the latter, with an organized garden layout where similar plants congregate in neat and tidy sections.

The garden entrance is through the restaurant or gift shop, where covered corridors stretch into the garden. If you're taking the self-guided tour, walk to the left, past flowering shrubs shaded by exotic trees, and soon you'll find yourself in the orchard. Noni, starfruit, lychee, cacao, avocado, sour sop and an abundance of citrus are just a few of the food plants you'll see growing here. The trail loops around past interesting trees like the sausage tree and cannonball tree, past a ginger grove and hibiscus planting to the center of the garden.

Orchids are the draw in this garden. Nani Mau's orchid pavilion is a covered display of hundreds, if not thousands, of flowering orchids planted amongst rock wall settings adorned with ferns and other epiphytes. There are even small cascading waterfalls incorporated into the architecture. The orchid display extends out from under cover, where delicate orchids cling to moss covered rock and hapu'u ferns sprout and reach for the sky.

The orchid display gives way to the hapu'u fern and anthurium display. From this planting, cross the main tram road and walk up a small hill to take in the entire garden from a lookout gazebo perched atop a verdant mound. This is a great spot to view the entire length of the stream that runs the width of the garden in the middle of a large clearing, east of the orchid pavilion.

left: Nani Mau Gardens has a large collection of hapu'u ferns. Some are planted in their own stand and others are mixed into the orchid pavilion. right: Golden bamboo and waterfall.

From the lookout, the tram road wraps around the stream, hugging the outskirts of the garden, denoted by tall Cook pines. The stream, a large open grass area and hapu'u grove comprises the entire east side of the garden. Stretching purple bougainvillea thrives on the stream's banks, hibiscus reaches for the sky and hala and coconut palms dot the surrounding landscape. As you continue around the stream, you'll find am open-air pavilion to get out of the sun or rain, depending on the weather.

At the origination point of the stream, a rocky, step-stone waterfall courses from the base of a wall of golden bamboo. A Japanese bell tower is perched on an adjoining rise. Ring the bell for luck. Behind the bell tower you'll find a small Japanese garden with stone bridges, black pine bonsai and flowering azalea bushes.

From there, the road wraps back up to the orchid pavilion. Before you depart, make sure you check out the bonsai display at the entrance to the garden by the restaurant.

left: Atop an elevated platform in the Japanese Garden, ring the bell for luck. right: The Japanese Garden blends structure, design and manicured trees.

Sadie Seymour Botanical Garden
(Kona Outdoor Educational Circle)

76-6280 Kuakini Highway, Kailua-Kona, Hawai'i 96740

Contact: (808) 326-7286 koc@konaoutdoorcircle.org www.konaoutdoorcircle.org

Directions: Located on the makai side of the intersection of Queen Ka'ahumanu Highway (Hwy 11) and Kuakini Highway (Hwy 11). From Ka'ahumanu Highway turn onto Kuakini Highway and keep left, heading toward the stop sign. Continue left and the Kona Outdoor Educational Circle is on the right.

Hours Daily: 9:00 a.m. to 5:00 p.m.

Admission: Free

Guided Hikes: Self-guided tours, but groups of 10 or more can request a docent by making a reservation in advance.

Facilities: Restrooms, educational center, drinking fountains.

Not a problem

30 inches

1.5 acres

Terraced landscaping

~300 feet

Level grass with stone steps

Slippers

This garden makes use of a long and narrow piece of property in a very unique way. The Sadie Seymour Botanical Garden, designed by community leader Sadie Seymour's son, landscape designer Scott Seymour, is organized into geographic plantings with the help of small and gradual stone terraces. With a steep incline on the mauka side of the garden and a serious grade on the makai side, the garden is a level botanical wedge, shaped like an arrowhead pointing north.

Tall trees and shrubs line both sides of the garden, but there are breaks in the foliage on the makai side that allow spectacular ocean views, adding to the calming effect of the garden. The terraces are planted with grass and palm trees, with most of the foliage located on the outer edges of the garden. This creates a valley between the foliage coming up

top left: The sections of the garden are broken up by the stone terraces. top right: A travelers palm is not a palm at all and is closely related to the Bird of Paradise. bottom: Palms are the real draw in this garden.

Hawai'i

Beyond the foliage is a breathtaking view of the Pacific.

all around and over you, isolating you from the bustling highway just up the hill and focusing your attention on the plants and tranquility at hand.

The plants growing in the well-manicured garden are a reflection of plants commonly grown in Hawai'i from around the world: Pacific Island, Austral, Indo-Malayan, Indo-Asian, Asian, Mediterranean, African, West Indian, South American, and Central American. The sections are quite small, just a handful of plants from each region, but the landscaping creates a seamless flow of foliage across the terraces, like a meandering stream.

Looking down upon the terraced garden from just beyond the visitor center.

At the top of the garden, the beginning of the walk, you'll find the native Hawaiian plants sections. Walk down the stairs and the entire garden is at your feet, a corridor of botanical samplings. Let the varying species of palms guide you down the terraces. The plants are not individually labeled, but instead one large sign calls out each section, listing the plants and pictorially showing their placement. It doesn't take long to reach the narrow tropical Central American nook at the far end of the garden, flanked with giant philodendron, heliconia and bromeliads, so take your time and make use of the benches to sit and enjoy the verdant foliage. With a host of tall exotic trees encircling the garden, it's a great locale to enjoy the shade in a beautiful garden setting.

Pottery adds a touch to the Mediterranean section.

University of Hawai'i at Hilo Botanical Garden

200 West Kawili Street, Hilo, Hawai'i 96720-4091

Contact: (808) 974-6200 hemmes@hawaii.edu

Directions: The Hawai'i Belt Road becomes Kanoelehua Avenue Turn onto E. Lanikaula Street heading mauka, or west. The garden is located on the corner of Nowelo Street and Lanikaula, near the upper entrance to the campus, across the street from the Church of the Holy Cross.

Hours Daily: Dawn to dark

Admission: Free

Guided Hikes: Contact Don Hemmes, Professor of Biology, for a guided tour.

Facilities: Restrooms and drinking fountains located on campus.

- Yes, and very aggressive
- ~150 inches
- Less than an acre
- Cycads
- ~150 feet
- Gravel paths
- Slippers

This small, but well manicured and maintained cycad, bromeliad and palm garden is well worth the visit. Don't let its size mask the variety of unique plants found here. To enter the garden, walk up the steps from Nowelo Street by the botanical garden sign, where brightly colored red, purple, yellow and orange bromeliads immediately catch your eye. The contrast of colors between the vibrant bromeliads, the deep green cycads and the black lava rocks that form the planting beds creates a prehistoric color palette, symbolic of the dominant plants in the garden—cycads.

Often confused with ferns or palms, but more closely related to pine trees because they produce cones that contain seeds, cycads were commonplace in the Triassic and Jurassic Periods, some 245 to 140 million years ago. Dating back to a time before flowering plants had evolved, cycads are now found in tropical and subtropical regions of the world.

Compare and contrast the myriad of bromeliads.

left: Palms, bromeliads and cycads all compliment and thrive in Hilo's moist climate. right: Cycads are often confused with ferns and palms, but produce seed-bearing cones and are more closely related to pine trees.

The collection of cycads at UH Hilo is extensive, with species hailing from Australia, North and Central America, Africa, China, Vietnam and Thailand. The thick and rigid, leafy plants produce cones that grow from the center of the leaf whorl. Since cycads produce both male and female cones, it's common to see the varying reproductive structures protruding or hanging from the center of the plants.

There is a greenhouse in the middle of the garden and several trails wind around the transparent structure. With the cycads meticulously planted with bromeliads and palms, the architecture of the garden produces a visual delight of texture and color. Juxtaposed by the slender trunks of native and exotic palms, there is a lot of horticulture packed into a small space.

The colorful leaves and flowers really pop against the black lava setting.

World Botanical Garden

P.O. Box 324, Honomu, Hawai'i 96728

Contact: (808) 963-5427 info@worldbotanicalgardens.com www.wbgi.com

Directions: From Highway 19, look for the sign near mile marker 16. Turn onto a paved road and follow the garden signs. At the stop sign at the top of the hill, turn right. The parking area and visitor center is just down the road on the right.

Hours Daily: 9:00 to 5:30 p.m.

Admission: $13 adults, $6 teens (13-17 years old), $3 children (5-12 years old), children under 5 years old are free. $6 kama'aina with I.D. Guided Tour: $40 adults, $30 teens (13-17 years old), $20 children (5-12 years old), children under 5 years of age are free.

Guided Hikes: Self-guided tours are available anytime, guided tours by Garden Director Lanny Neel are offered by reservations only and include lunch. Call (808) 896-9434.

Facilities: Visitor center, restrooms, picnic area, snacks and beverages.

There's good reason why the repellent is offered at the visitor center

~110 inches

275 acres

Diversity of plants and Umauma Falls

~300 feet

Level concrete paths and grass

Shoes

World Botanical Gardens is an expansive natural complex, complete with botanical gardens, a three-tier waterfall, orchard and rainforest trail. It's no wonder why every paid admission to the garden is good for visiting many times over for up to one week, so make sure to save your admission slip.

The Hamakua Coast is known for its deep ravines and waterfalls, and this garden showcases a prime example of the power of water. From the visitor center you'll be instructed to drive about a mile back into the property, to the beautiful Umauma Falls. There is a lookout from the roadside at a 500-foot elevation that offers unobstructed views of this three-tiered fall rushing through a verdant, forested valley. The falls are quite a ways below in the gorge, so there's no going for a swim, but the photo-ops are

left: Umauma Falls from the lookout. right: Orchids cling to branches and trunks throughout the garden. Here, a cattleya ochids blossoms on a citrus tree.

a golden opportunity. A stand of eucalyptus trees blankets the ridgeline in the far off distance above the falls.

Hop back in the car and continue down the road another half mile. When you come to an intersection, there's a small gravel parking area. This is the trailhead to the rainforest trail. The trail follows the perennial Honopueo Stream under a canopy of mature trees and tropical foliage. The three-quarter mile walk traverses along the gulch's edge, forested with tropical and subtropical plants from around the world, some of which you'll find in the garden and others that are only found along the trail. When you reach the end of the trail, you can follow the trail back to your car or walk along a dirt road that skirts an old sugarcane field.

The actual botanical gardens are back behind the visitor center, where fresh fruit from the garden is offered up throughout the day. There is a path that circumnavigates the rain-fed garden, but feel free to roam anywhere you want. Get up close and personal with the plants: touching and tasting, when you know it's safe, is encouraged. Started back in 1995, the garden is an eclectic collection of botanicals from around the world. Economic plants like cotton, stevia, allspice and cinnamon are threaded around plantings of ginger, croton and heliconia and other flowering shrubs. Palms and exotic canopy trees like champaca, royal Poinciana and red powder puff are just a few examples of the ornate foliage and flowers overhead.

There are so many interesting and unique plants growing in this garden—pencil tree, blue sandpaper vine, tropical rhododendrons, sexy pink heliconia—it's hard to see them all unless you know what you're looking for. That being the

top left: Appropriately named sexy pink ginger. top right: Pineapple ginger with edible yellow flowers. bottom left: Just because there is a paved path doesn't mean you have to stay on it. bottom right: The garden is thick with understory plants and it is encouraged that you wander around anywhere you like.

case, the best possible way to explore the botanical garden is with the garden director, Dr. Lanny Neel. If you're keen to try new things, Lanny is sure to point out the intricacies of all his plants using all your senses, especially taste.

The garden also features a mock orange hedge maze, a cactus and succulent garden with agave and yucca and a small orchard. Follow the row of Cook pines away from the visitor center, past the citrus scent of the lemon eucalyptus trees for a beautiful view of the ocean. In this garden, orchids and ferns adorn the trunks and crotches of trees, fruit is plentiful and something is always in bloom.

The garden is also home to many types of succulents and many varieties of agave, including the massive century agave.

Glossary of Terms

Aerial roots – adventitious above-ground roots.

Ahupua'a – ancient Hawaiian system of land division and resource management extending from the highest point in the mountains into the ocean.

Botanical garden – gardens holding documented collections of living plants for the purpose of scientific research, conservation, display and education.

Canoe plants – 24 important plants the first Polynesian settlers carried in their canoes and planted across the Hawaiian Islands.

Canopy – refers to the outer most layer of leaves of a single tree or the uppermost layer of trees in a forest that shields the forest floor from sun, wind and the deteriorating effects of hard rain.

Cultivar – shorthand for "cultivated variety." They are distinct varieties of plants maintained in cultivation by human efforts. They are of hybrid origin or varieties of plants that occur in the wild.

Endangered – a species of plant that is at an extremely high risk of becoming extinct due to declining population or threatened by loss of habitat or predation.

Endemic – a plant that is found in one area only and nowhere else.

Epiphyte – a plant that grows on another plant for support, but takes no nourishment from the host plant, living on nutrients drawn from the air, rainwater and organic debris.

Exceptional Trees – designated by reason of age, rarity, location, size, aesthetic quality, endemic status or historical and cultural significance by the County Arborist Committee as worthy of preservation. The Exceptional Trees Ordinance Act 105 was enacted by the Hawai'i State Legislature in 1975.

Exotic – plants brought to Hawai'i after the arrival of Europeans, also called introduced.

Heiau – pre-Christian place of worship, shrine.

Honolulu Botanical Gardens – five botanical gardens located in the County of Honolulu on O'ahu and operated by the county.

Hybrid – a distinct plant resulting from a cross between two species, subspecies, varieties, cultivars, strains, or any combination of the above, most often produced by plant breeders.

Indigenous – a plant that arrived in Hawai'i without human assistance, but is also found elsewhere.

Inflorescence – a group of individual flowers on a single stem that can take many forms.

Invasive – fast growing and easily spreading non-native introduced plants that outcompete and overpower native plants.

Makai – ocean.

Mauka – mountain.

National Tropical Botanical Gardens – four botanical gardens and three preserves in Hawai'i with one botanical garden in Florida; the only botanical garden with a charter from the United States Congress.

Native – plants that reached Hawai'i either by wind, wing or water, without the aid of humans.

Palmetum – a collection of many different species of palms from around the world.

Pollinator – a biotic agent (insect, bat, bird) that moves pollen from the male anthers of a flower to the female stigma of a flower to accomplish fertilization.

Polynesian introductions – plants brought to Hawai'i by the migrating people of Polynesia, from about A.D. 200 to A.D. 1300.

Rare – plants with less than 50 individuals remaining in the wild.

Riparian – plant communities along the banks of rivers and streams.

Seed bank – a type of gene bank and conservation strategy; a seed bank stores viable seeds for up to 30 years as a source for growing and planting rare and endangered plants.

Slippers – term used in Hawai'i for simple footwear also known as sandals, thongs or flip-flops.

Subtropical – the zones of the Earth immediately north and south of the tropic zone.

Tropical – meaning "near the equator," the equatorial regions of the world between the Tropic of Cancer in the northern hemisphere and the Tropic of Capricorn in the southern hemisphere.

Tuff ring - a wide, low-rimmed, well-bedded accumulation of hyalo-clastic debris built around a volcanic vent; the classic volcano cone shape.

Xeriscape – a gardening technique based on water conservation through proper landscaping, taking advantage of water thrifty plants, mulching and natural climate conditions to make efficient use of irrigation.

Bibliography

————. *The Amy B.H. Greenwell Ethnobotanical Garden*. Honolulu: Bishop Museum Press.

Carr, Gerald D. *Campus Plants*. Honolulu: Office of University Relations, 1991.

Choy, Duane. "Discover Contemporary Museum's gardens." *Honolulu Advertiser*, Friday, July 6, 2007.

————. *Foster Botanical Garden*. Honolulu: City and County of Honolulu, Department of Parks and Recreation, 2007.

Hall, John B. *A Hiker's Guide to Trailside Plants In Hawai'i*. Honolulu: Mutual Publishing, 2004.

"Hawai'i's Botanical and Other Public Gardens." http://www.hawaii.edu/sciref/botgarden.html

————. *Hawai'i Tropical Botanical Garden*. Pāpa'ikou, Hawai'i: Hawai'i Tropical Botanical Garden, 1994.

"Honolulu Botanical Gardens." http://www.honolulu.gov/parks/hbg/

————. *Ho'omaluhia Botanical Garden*. Honolulu: City and County of Honolulu, Department of Parks and Recreation, 2006.

————. *Kahanu Garden*. Kalaheo, Hawai'i: National Tropical Botanical Garden.

Leaser, David. *Growing Palm Trees In Hawai'i And Other Tropical Climates*. Honolulu: Mutual Publishing, 2007.

————. *Limahuli Garden: A Window To Ancient Hawai'i*. Kalaheo, Hawai'i: National Tropical Botanical Garden: 2008.

————. *Manuka*. Hilo: State of Hawai'i, Department of Land and Natural Resources Natural Area Reserve Systems.

————. *Maui Nui Botanical Gardens*. Kahului: Maui Nui Botanical Gardens, 2007.

"National Tropical Botanical Garden." http://www.ntbg.org/

————. *Plantation Manor and Moir Pa'u a Laka: The Story of Kiahuna Plantation's Cactus and Flower Garden.*: Outrigger Kiahuna Plantation, 2008.

Pratt, H. Douglas. *A Pocket Guide to Hawai'i's Trees and Shrubs*. Honolulu: Mutual Publishing, 1998.

Tsutsumi, Cheryl Chee. "Waimea Falls Park gets back to its roots." *Star-Bulletin*, Sunday, January 13, 2002.

————. *Wahiawa Botanical Garden*. Honolulu: City and County of Honolulu, Department of Parks and Recreation, 2006.

————. *Western Garden Book*. California: Sunset Publishing, 2001.

About the Author

Kevin J. Whitton is the editor of *Green: Hawai'i's Sustainable Living Magazine*, editor for *FreeSurf Magazine* on the North Shore of O'ahu, contributing writer to the *Honolulu Weekly* and freelance writer to regional, national and international publications. An avid naturalist and botanical hobbyist, he is also the author of  *Green Hawai'i: A Guide to a Sustainable and Energy Efficient Home*, a 2009 Ka Palapala Po'okela award winning book and *Rain, Beans and Rice: Memoirs of Life in a Costa Rican Rain Forest*, an adventure travel memoir based on his three-month experience as a trail guide in a private rainforest preserve. He holds a B.A. of Sociology from the University of California, Santa Barbara and has lived in California, Colorado, Costa Rica and Australia. He resides with his wife, their baby daughter and two cats on the windward side of O'ahu.

ISBN-10: 1-56647-861-8
ISBN-13: 978-1-56647-861-8
6.75"x9" softcover 128pp.
$16.95

Green Hawaiʻi: *A Guide to a Sustainable and Energy Efficient Home* is an easy-to-use reference that explores many of the ways anyone in Hawaiʻi can make their home a more energy-efficient and sustainable place to live. Packed with facts and figures, personal anecdotes, and suggestions from authorities in the field, this book is a valuable tool whether you want to install a solar hot-water heating system, plant a tree to shade and cool your home, or get a community recycling bin at your local school. Put it in your pocket and take it with you to the hardware store, or leave it on the coffee table to invite discussion and interest; either way, it is a must-read for Island residents.